CONTENTS

Published 2009. Pedigree Books, Beech Hill House, Walnut Gardens, Exeter, Devon, EX4 4DH.
books@pedigreegroup.co.uk | www.pedigreebooks.com
Written by Rachel Elliot | Photographs © FremantleMedia, Ken McKay, Jack Davis and Sarah Gouk.
Pedigree Books would like to thank Jack Davis and Sarah Gouk for their help in compiling this book.
Copyright © FremantleMedia Limited 2009
The X Factor is a trademark of FremantleMedia Limited and Simco Limited.
Licensed by FremantleMedia Enterprises. www.fremantlemedia.com

Welcome to this sizzling celebration of the UK's most dynamic entertainment show! With a record-breaking number of applicants and a brand-new audition process, the 2009 search for the next singing superstar is the biggest and most explosive ever.

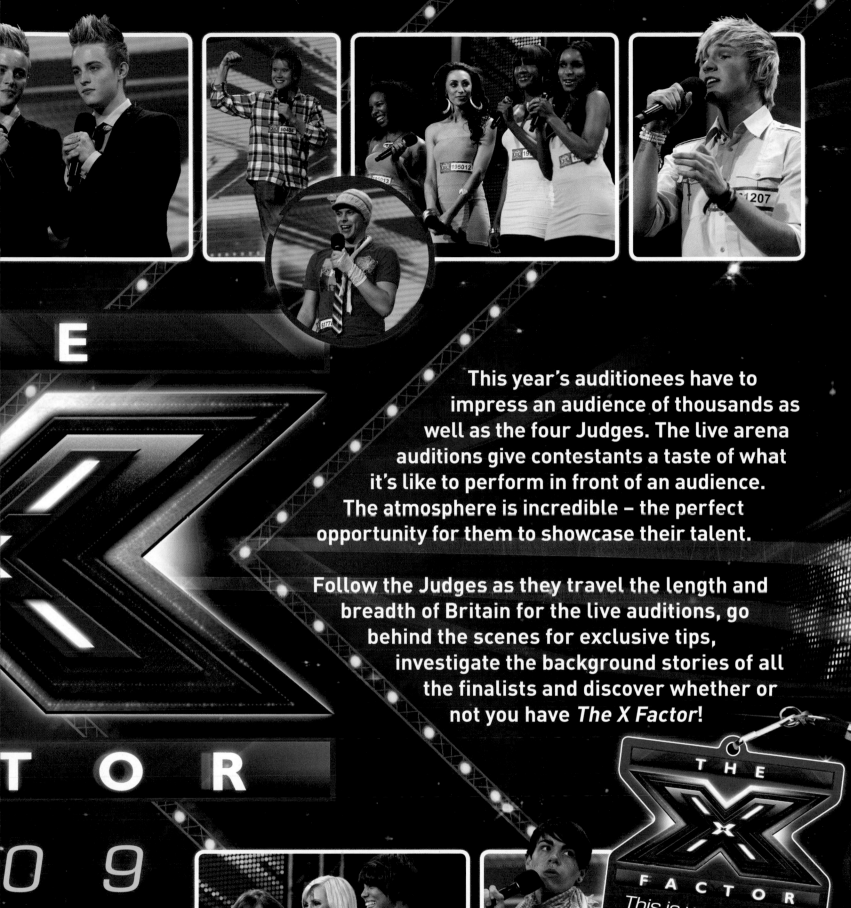

This year's auditionees have to impress an audience of thousands as well as the four Judges. The live arena auditions give contestants a taste of what it's like to perform in front of an audience. The atmosphere is incredible – the perfect opportunity for them to showcase their talent.

Follow the Judges as they travel the length and breadth of Britain for the live auditions, go behind the scenes for exclusive tips, investigate the background stories of all the finalists and discover whether or not you have *The X Factor*!

THE

X

FACTOR

This is your access-all-areas pass to the ultimate TV spectacle!

Your name:

① The Golden Ticket

The path to stardom is strewn with obstacles the contestants will have to overcome if they are going to succeed. Of course, if they've got the X Factor, they're sure to rise to the challenge!

② Auditions

The auditions are the first step on the way to making dreams come true. Contestants will stand in front of Cheryl Cole, Simon Cowell, Dannii Minogue and Louis Walsh, and try to convince the four Judges that they have what it takes to win *The X Factor*.

The big surprise for this year's contestants is that they will be auditioning in front of a live audience. Emotions will be running high as the acts face the toughest audition process yet!

Each act must do everything he or she can to dazzle the Judges . . . and the audience! The Judges work together at this stage of the competition, and contestants will have to get a 'Yes' from at least three of them to make it through to Bootcamp.

③ Bootcamp

At Bootcamp, contestants will find themselves onstage in front of a live audience once again! This is their chance to show the Judges that they have confidence, audience appeal and talent. They only have one chance to get it right, so they have to seize the day!

The Judges work together to pick their favourite contestants from each of the four categories to take to the next stage of the competition – Judges' Houses. At the end of Bootcamp, each Judge is given a category to mentor.

④ Judges' Houses

From this point on, the pressure really starts to build. The Judges work one-to-one with their assigned acts. At the end of this stage, each Judge will pick his or her three favourite acts to take part in the live studio shows.

⑤ The Live Shows

From now on the shows are broadcast live every week, and this is where the public gets involved! Every week the audience at home will vote for their favourite of the twelve finalists. In the results show, the two acts with the lowest public vote will sing once again. Then it will be up to the Judges to decide who they think should stay in the competition and who should go home.

Who do *you* predict will have the determination, talent and star quality to win this year's *The X Factor?*

WINNER 2009

"There are a few people who actually want to **GO BACK TO SCHOOL** now because of you!"
Dannii

935

Danyl Johnson

DANYL LOVES TEACHING AND IS HUGELY PROUD OF ALL HIS STUDENTS, BUT HIS TRUE PASSION IS MUSIC AND PERFORMING. HE FEELS THAT HE BELONGS ON STAGE, AND HE WANTS TO SHOW THE AUDIENCE OF *THE X FACTOR* THAT HE IS A SUPERSTAR IN THE MAKING. IN HIS SPARE TIME HE SINGS AND WRITES SONGS FOR HIS OWN BAND, AND HE LOVES FOOTBALL, TENNIS AND GOLF. HE'S CERTAINLY NOT AFRAID OF HARD WORK!

"That was single-handedly **THE BEST FIRST AUDITION** I have ever heard."
Simon

"**I THANK GOD** that you came in today."
Louis

Danyl lit up the stage with his audition performance, and he has continued to light up *The X Factor* ever since. He's hoping that he can carry his spark through to the final and become the winner of *The X Factor* 2009!

PROFILE

AGE:	27
HOME TOWN:	READING
JOB:	TEACHER
AUDITION CITY:	LONDON
MENTOR:	SIMON

SONG CHOICES

AUDITION:
'WITH A LITTLE HELP FROM MY FRIENDS'

BOOTCAMP:
'HOLDING BACK THE YEARS'

BE THE FIFTH JUDGE! JOIN THE JUDGING PANEL AND MAKE SOME PREDICTIONS!

BEST PERFORMANCE:	
WEAKEST MOMENT:	
YOUR FAVOURITES POLL:	/12
DEPARTURE WEEK:	
DOES DANYL HAVE THE X FACTOR?	
YOUR X FACTOR SCORE:	/10

"You're a **NATURAL PERFORMER.**"

Louis

Olly Murs

DURING THE DAY, OLLY GIVES PEOPLE ADVICE ON HOW TO SAVE MONEY ON THEIR ENERGY BILLS. BUT HE DREAMS OF SWAPPING HIS TELEPHONE FOR A MICROPHONE AND EARNING HIS LIVING AS A SINGER. NOW HE HAS A CHANCE TO MAKE THAT DREAM COME TRUE!

PROFILE

AGE:	25
HOME TOWN:	WITHAM
JOB:	OFFICE WORKER
AUDITION CITY:	LONDON
MENTOR:	SIMON

SONG CHOICES

AUDITION:
'SUPERSTITION'

BOOTCAMP:
'YOUR SONG'

BE THE FIFTH JUDGE!
JOIN THE JUDGING PANEL AND MAKE SOME PREDICTIONS!

BEST PERFORMANCE: _____

WEAKEST MOMENT: _____

YOUR FAVOURITES POLL: **/12**

DEPARTURE WEEK: _____

DOES OLLY HAVE THE X FACTOR? _____

YOUR X FACTOR SCORE: **/10**

BOOTCAMP

Olly enjoys football and socializing, but more than anything else he loves singing. His dream is to be famous, sell records and be an international superstar.

Olly sings in front of the mirror and at family parties, but performing in front of the live audience at his audition was a whole new challenge! However, he soon had the audience cheering and singing along and, at the end, even Simon was applauding. The enthusiastic reaction left Olly lost for words! More than anything, he wants to keep entertaining the audience and prove that he has the X Factor.

BOOTCAMP

"You're very, **VERY COOL.**"
Simon

FIRST AUDITION

"You've got some soul **IN YOUR VOICE.**"
Cheryl

FIRST AUDITION

"THANK YOU
for coming to the auditions!"
Dannii

Jamie 'Afro' Archer

JAMIE HAS SPENT YEARS PLAYING IN PUBS AND CLUBS, BUT HAS NEVER MANAGED TO BREAK INTO THE BIG TIME... UNTIL NOW! *THE X FACTOR* HAS GIVEN HIM THE CHANCE TO GIVE THE KIND OF PERFORMANCES HE HAS ALWAYS KNOWN WERE INSIDE HIM. HIS LOVE OF MUSIC IS CLEAR – IT SHINES OUT OF HIM LIKE A LIGHT. AT HIS AUDITION, HE EVEN HAD SIMON SINGING ALONG!

PROFILE

AGE:	33	**SONG CHOICES**	
HOME TOWN:	LONDON	AUDITION:	
JOB:	MUSICIAN	'SEX ON FIRE'	
AUDITION CITY:	LONDON		
MENTOR:	SIMON	BOOTCAMP:	
		'WITH OR WITHOUT YOU'	

BE THE FIFTH JUDGE!
JOIN THE JUDGING PANEL AND MAKE SOME PREDICTIONS!

BEST PERFORMANCE:

WEAKEST MOMENT:

YOUR FAVOURITES POLL: /12

DEPARTURE WEEK:

DOES JAMIE HAVE THE X FACTOR?

YOUR X FACTOR SCORE: /10

Jamie's confidence had been knocked over the years, and he knew that this chance could be his last. He successfully sang his way through Bootcamp and Simon chose to put him through the live shows. Now he has to show that his natural gift for entertaining can carry him all the way to the top!

"Natural born ENTERTAINER."
Cheryl

"You know what I like about you, James? YOU'RE FEARLESS!"
Simon

"It was a real SURPRISE!"

Stacey Soloman

STACEY IS A STUDENT AND SINGLE MOTHER FROM ESSEX, WHO HAS DREAMED OF HAVING A SINGING CAREER ALL HER LIFE. HER SON IS HER INSPIRATION AND HER DRIVING FORCE; SHE IS DETERMINED TO GIVE HIM A WONDERFUL LIFE, AND HOPES THAT *THE X FACTOR* WILL HELP HER TO SUCCEED.

"I think you are really,

REALLY GOOD."
Simon

"**THIS MEANS
EVERYTHING**
to me!" Stacey

She amazed the Judges with her heartfelt rendition of 'What A Wonderful World' and sailed through to Bootcamp. Her powerful performances carried her on to the next stage, and eventually Dannii picked her to perform on the live shows. With a glittering future almost within touching distance, can Stacey make her dreams come true?

PROFILE

AGE:	19	**SONG CHOICES**
HOME TOWN:	DAGENHAM	**AUDITION:** 'WHAT A WONDERFUL WORLD'
JOB:	STUDENT	
AUDITION CITY:	LONDON	**BOOTCAMP:** 'THERE YOU'LL BE'
MENTOR:	DANNII	

BE THE FIFTH JUDGE! JOIN THE JUDGING PANEL AND MAKE SOME PREDICTIONS!

BEST PERFORMANCE:

WEAKEST MOMENT:

YOUR FAVOURITES POLL: /12

DEPARTURE WEEK:

DOES STACEY HAVE THE X FACTOR?

YOUR X FACTOR SCORE: /10

"**THIS IS MY DREAM;** I've never wanted to do anything else."
Lucie

61524

Lucie Jones

LUCIE COMES FROM A SMALL VILLAGE JUST OUTSIDE CARDIFF. EVERYONE IN THE VILLAGE IS SUPPORTING HER AND WISHING HER WELL! DESPITE HER RURAL UPBRINGING, LUCIE HAS HER EYES ON THE BRIGHT LIGHTS. HER AMBITION IS TO LEAVE HER CHILDHOOD HOME BEHIND AND STEP ONTO THE BIG STAGE, WHERE SHE FEELS SHE TRULY BELONGS.

"I LOVED
the vulnerability in
your performance."

Cheryl

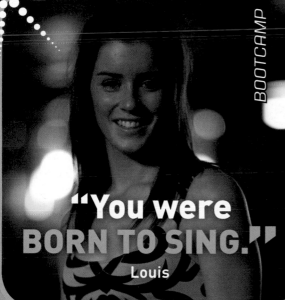

**"You were
BORN TO SING."**

Louis

Lucie poured emotion into her audition
song, and her performance hugely
impressed the Judges. She has made
it through the rigorous early stages,
but can she keep delivering stunning
performances week after week on the
live shows? Only time will tell!

PROFILE

AGE:	18	SONG CHOICES
HOME TOWN:	PENTRYCH	AUDITION: 'I WILL ALWAYS LOVE YOU'
JOB:	STUDENT	
AUDITION CITY:	CARDIFF	BOOTCAMP: 'HURT'
MENTOR:	DANNII	

BE THE FIFTH JUDGE! JOIN THE JUDGING PANEL AND MAKE SOME PREDICTIONS!

BEST PERFORMANCE:	
WEAKEST MOMENT:	
YOUR FAVOURITES POLL:	/12
DEPARTURE WEEK:	
DOES LUCIE HAVE THE X FACTOR?	
YOUR X FACTOR SCORE:	/10

"Absolutely YES!"
Louis

Rachel Adedeji

RACHEL FIRST AUDITIONED IN 2008, BUT SHE DIDN'T MAKE IT PAST THE EARLY STAGES OF THE COMPETITION. HOWEVER, WITH TRUE DETERMINATION SHE RETURNED TO TRY AGAIN. THE JUDGES RECOGNISED HER AS SHE WALKED ONTO THE STAGE AND PRAISED HER FOR HAVING THE COURAGE TO COME BACK.

PROFILE

AGE:	18	**SONG CHOICES**
HOME TOWN:	LONDON	**AUDITION:**
JOB:	STUDENT	'AIN'T NO MOUNTAIN HIGH ENOUGH'
AUDITION CITY:	LONDON	**BOOTCAMP:**
MENTOR:	DANNII	'LAST REQUEST'

BE THE FIFTH JUDGE! JOIN THE JUDGING PANEL AND MAKE SOME PREDICTIONS!

BEST PERFORMANCE:

WEAKEST MOMENT:

YOUR FAVOURITES POLL: /12

DEPARTURE WEEK:

DOES RACHEL HAVE THE X FACTOR?

YOUR X FACTOR SCORE: /10

Rachel agreed that the Judges had made the right decision in 2008, because it had taught her to control her nerves.

Her beautiful voice took her through to the Judges' Houses stage, and this time Dannii picked her to perform on the live shows. Now she feels ready to face an audience of thousands!

"Here we **GO** again!"
Simon

"Welcome back – **YES!**"
Cheryl

"You've just made the competition get very, very EXCITING."

Louis

Joseph McElderry

JOSEPH STARTED SINGING FOUR YEARS AGO. HE GOT UP AND PERFORMED KARAOKE ONE DAY, AND DISCOVERED THAT HE HAD A VOICE! HE LOVES ENTERTAINING PEOPLE AND GETS A HUGE KICK OUT OF SEEING THEM ENJOY HIS PERFORMANCE.

PROFILE

AGE:	18
HOME TOWN:	SOUTH SHIELDS
JOB:	STUDENT
AUDITION CITY:	MANCHESTER
MENTOR:	CHERYL

SONG CHOICES

AUDITION:
'DANCE WITH MY FATHER'

BOOTCAMP:
'PRAYING FOR TIME'

BE THE FIFTH JUDGE! JOIN THE JUDGING PANEL AND MAKE SOME PREDICTIONS!

BEST PERFORMANCE:

WEAKEST MOMENT:

YOUR FAVOURITES POLL: /12

DEPARTURE WEEK:

DOES JOSEPH HAVE THE X FACTOR?

YOUR X FACTOR SCORE: /10

His stunning first audition drew cheers from the crowd and admiration from the Judges. His family was waiting eagerly in the wings, and Joseph couldn't wait to share his excitement with them!

Joseph wants to succeed in music and make his parents proud. This opportunity could change his life forever – has he got what it takes to reach the final?

"I'm really proud you're REPRESENTING our city."
Cheryl

"We may just have found ourselves A POP STAR."
Simon

"I love the fact that **YOU'VE COME BACK FIGHTING** ...you've got the X Factor for me."
Louis

Rikki Loney

RIKKI LONEY RETURNED TO *THE X FACTOR* THIS YEAR AFTER BEING TURNED DOWN IN 2008. HE HOPES THAT HE CAN PROVE THAT THE JUDGES WERE WAS WRONG LAST YEAR!

"Your mum's going to be so **PROUD!**"
Dannii

"You could be Scotland's **HIGHEST HOPE** in the competition."
Simon

BOOTCAMP

BOOTCAMP

BOOTCAMP

PROFILE

AGE:	21	**SONG CHOICES**
HOME TOWN:	DENNISTOUN	**AUDITION:** 'THESE ARMS OF MINE'
JOB:	RECRUITMENT	
AUDITION CITY:	GLASGOW	**BOOTCAMP:** 'CHASING PAVEMENTS'
MENTOR:	CHERYL	

BE THE FIFTH JUDGE! JOIN THE JUDGING PANEL AND MAKE SOME PREDICTIONS!

BEST PERFORMANCE:

WEAKEST MOMENT:

YOUR FAVOURITES POLL: /12

DEPARTURE WEEK:

DOES RIKKI HAVE THE X FACTOR?

YOUR X FACTOR SCORE: /10

Since narrowly missing out on getting through Bootcamp last year, Rikki has been singing in pubs and social clubs, improving his skills and his confidence. He dreams of performing in his own concerts and singing on the big stage. He has never wanted anything so much!

Rikki was so nervous about re-auditioning, he didn't even tell his mother that he was coming! But he is passionate about music, and he is determined to work harder than he has ever worked before to make his dreams come true!

"You're the first person I'm going to say 'YOU'VE GOT THE X FACTOR' to."
Cheryl

Lloyd Daniels

BEFORE AUDITIONING FOR *THE X FACTOR*, LLOYD HAD ONLY EVER PERFORMED IN SCHOOL PLAYS. IT WAS VERY DAUNTING FOR HIM TO STAND IN FRONT OF THE JUDGES AND THE AUDIENCE AND PERFORM. HE HAD A SHAKY START IN HIS AUDITION, AND FOR A MOMENT IT LOOKED AS IF HE MIGHT HAVE BLOWN HIS CHANCES. BUT THE JUDGES GAVE HIM THE CHANCE TO START AGAIN, AND THIS TIME HE USED HIS TWO MINUTES TO DEVASTATING EFFECT!

BOOTCAMP

FIRST AUDITION

"You took the nerves and put them into THE PERFORMANCE."
Dannii

BOOTCAMP

"It was AMAZING!"
Lloyd

Lloyd sailed through Bootcamp and Cheryl chose to put him through to the live shows. Now the opportunity of a lifetime is being handed to him – can he seize it?

PROFILE

AGE: 16

FROM: SOUTH WALES

JOB: STUDENT

AUDITION CITY: CARDIFF

MENTOR: CHERYL

SONG CHOICES

AUDITION:
'TURN BACK THE HANDS OF TIME'

BOOTCAMP:
'YOU ARE NOT ALONE'

BE THE FIFTH JUDGE! JOIN THE JUDGING PANEL AND MAKE SOME PREDICTIONS!

BEST PERFORMANCE:

WEAKEST MOMENT:

YOUR FAVOURITES POLL: /12

DEPARTURE WEEK:

DOES LLOYD HAVE THE X FACTOR?

YOUR X FACTOR SCORE: /10

"I absolutely **LOVE THIS GIRL!**"

Simon

Miss Frank

MISS F.R.A.N.K. DIDN'T START OFF AS A GROUP! THEY AUDITIONED SEPARATELY, BUT AT BOOTCAMP THE JUDGES SUGGESTED THAT THEY SHOULD TEAM UP… AND WHAT A RESULT! TOGETHER THEY POWERED THROUGH TO THE JUDGES' HOUSES STAGE, AND FINALLY LOUIS DECIDED THAT THEY SHOULD REPRESENT HIM IN THE LIVE SHOWS.

"I really ENJOYED IT!"
Cheryl

PROFILE

AGE:	21-25	SONG CHOICES:	
HOME TOWN:	LONDON	AUDITION: BAND NOT FORMED	
AUDITION CITY:	LONDON		
MENTOR:	LOUIS	BOOTCAMP: 'WISHING ON A STAR'	

BE THE FIFTH JUDGE! JOIN THE JUDGING PANEL AND MAKE SOME PREDICTIONS!

BEST PERFORMANCE:

WEAKEST MOMENT:

YOUR FAVOURITES POLL: /12

DEPARTURE WEEK:

DO MISS FRANK HAVE THE X FACTOR?

YOUR X FACTOR SCORE: /10

Graziella Affinita, Shanice Davis and Shar Alexander are fresh and new, and ready to show the UK that they have what it takes to win *The X Factor*!

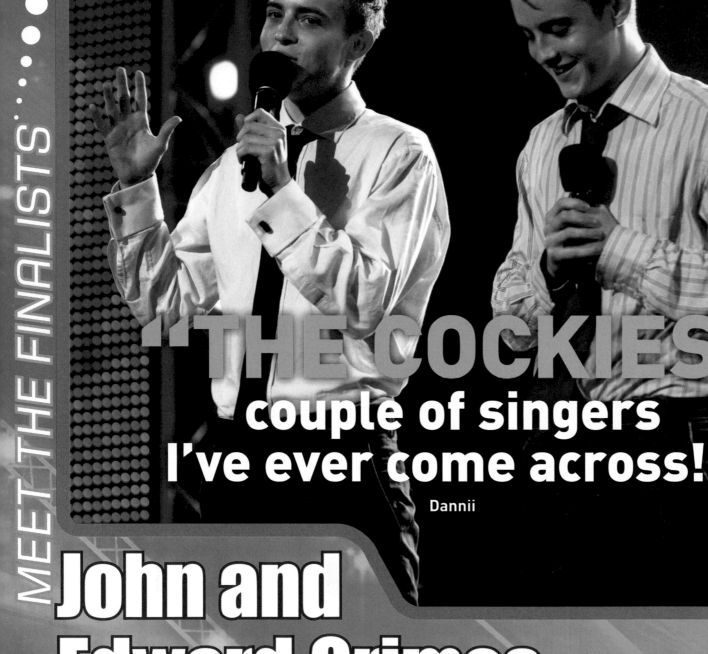

"THE COCKIEST
couple of singers
I've ever come across!"
Dannii

John and Edward Grimes

JOHN AND EDWARD MIGHT BE SOME OF THE YOUNGEST CONTESTANTS IN THE COMPETITION, BUT THEY ARE BRIMMING WITH CONFIDENCE! THEY HAVEN'T BEEN TO STAGE SCHOOL OR HAD ANY VOCAL TRAINING, SO THEY ARE RELYING ON PURE, NATURAL TALENT TO CARRY THEM THROUGH TO THE FINAL. IT'S WORKED SO FAR!

"**There's something INTRIGUING about you.**"
Cheryl

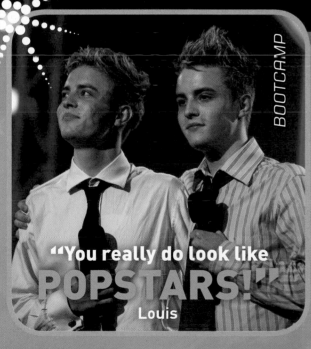

"**You really do look like POPSTARS!**"
Louis

The boys plan to make their live performances even more extravagant with plenty of fun twists and dance moves. They are improving all the time and feel that they have lots more to give. Simon isn't a fan so far, but now John and Edward have the chance to make him change his mind about them. Can they do it?

PROFILE

AGE:	17	**SONG CHOICES**
HOME TOWN:	DUBLIN	**AUDITION:**
JOB:	STUDENTS	'AS LONG AS YOU LOVE ME'
AUDITION CITY:	GLASGOW	**BOOTCAMP:**
MENTOR:	LOUIS	'YOU ARE NOT ALONE'

BE THE FIFTH JUDGE! JOIN THE JUDGING PANEL AND MAKE SOME PREDICTIONS!

BEST PERFORMANCE:

WEAKEST MOMENT:

YOUR FAVOURITES POLL: /12

DEPARTURE WEEK:

DO JOHN AND EDWARD HAVE THE X FACTOR?

YOUR X FACTOR SCORE: /10

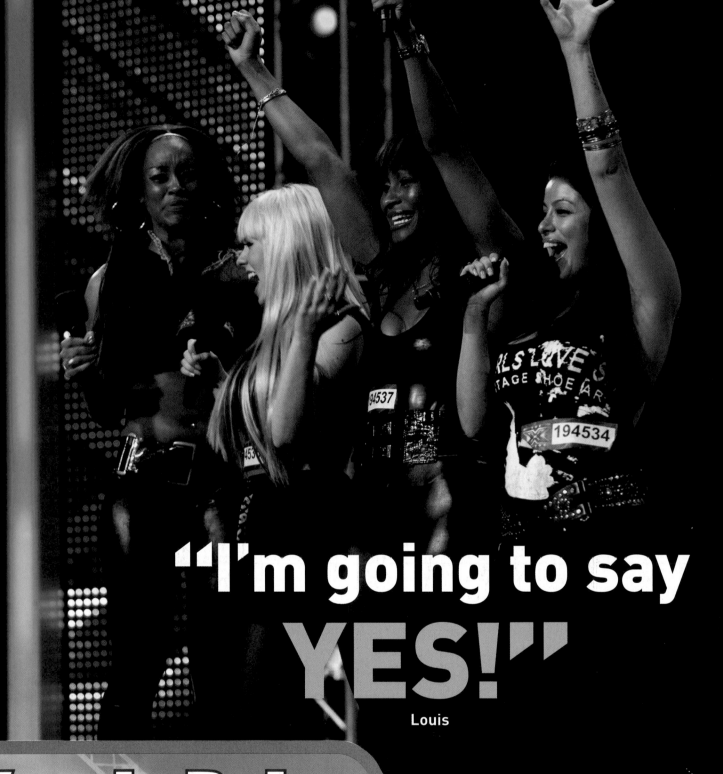

"I'm going to say YES!"

Louis

Kandy Rain

KANDY RAIN IS MADE UP OF BEST FRIENDS AZI, COCO, CHEMMANE AND KHATEREH. THE GIRLS ARE SASSY, STYLISH AND SIMPLY SENSATIONAL. THEIR AMBITION IS TO CHANGE THE FACE OF BRITISH POP, AND THEY ARE HEADING FOR THE BIG TIME. THEIR AUDITION BOWLED OVER THE JUDGES, AND NOW THEY HOPE THAT THEIR VOICES, DANCING AND IMAGE WILL IMPRESS THE BRITISH PUBLIC JUST AS MUCH.

PROFILE

AGE: 21-25

HOME TOWN: DUBLIN, HITCHIN, BASINGSTOKE, LONDON

JOB: DANCE TEACHER, MODEL, SALON WORKER, SINGER

AUDITION CITY: LONDON

MENTOR: LOUIS

SONG CHOICES:

AUDITION: 'DON'T CHA'

BOOTCAMP: 'IF YOU LOVE ME'

BE THE FIFTH JUDGE! JOIN THE JUDGING PANEL AND MAKE SOME PREDICTIONS!

BEST PERFORMANCE:

WEAKEST MOMENT:

YOUR FAVOURITES POLL: /12

DEPARTURE WEEK:

DO KANDY RAIN HAVE THE X FACTOR?

YOUR X FACTOR SCORE: /10

The girls met at an audition for *The X Factor*, and instantly felt a bond. They are very close and their chemistry feeds their energy and ambition. Together they are determined to win the 2009 competition and make all their dreams come true!

"You girls are SEXY"

Dannii

33

Behind the Scenes

This is your chance to get a sneak peek at how *The X Factor* is put together. Meet the line producer and find out exactly what happens behind the scenes of your favourite show!

What is your job on The X Factor?

It is my job to co-ordinate all the aspects of the show. I have to make sure everything is organised and runs smoothly, and that everyone knows what he or she is supposed to be doing!

Who organises and plans the filming of the contestants during the week?

Filming throughout the week is mainly organised by the assistant producers. They have a minute-by-minute schedule of what the contestants are up to, so they can get the most interesting and exciting shots.

When do the rehearsals take place?

Studio rehearsals take place on Friday and Saturday. There is also a sound check on Friday afternoon or evening in the studio. We have to double-check everything that could affect the live show!

Who turns up for the rehearsals?

Everyone! The contestants, the crew, the producers, the vocal coaches, the choreography team, the dancers and even the Judges . . . everyone needs to know the running order of the show.

What happens in the run-up to a live show?

At the start of the week, the contestants are given their songs and rehearsals begin. The week is spent vocal coaching, perfecting choreography and going for wardrobe fittings. Contestants are also filmed all through the week. There is a studio dress rehearsal on the Friday before the show. It's a very busy week for the contestants – and for me!

Contestants work hard to memorise their choreography during the week so they know exactly what to do on the live show.

How many rehearsals do the contestants get on the stage?

They rehearse three times on Friday night at the sound check, two or three times on Saturday morning at camera rehearsal and one or two times on Saturday afternoon during dress rehearsal.

Who decides on the lighting, camera shots and special effects for each performance?

Naturally, the Judges have opinions about how each act's performance should be presented. The whole team discusses all the elements of each performance, including dancers, backing singers, choirs, special effects and props. When the Judges, the contestants and the team are happy with the plan, the studio director will put it into action. ↘

The all-important vocal coaching is captured on film.

Behind the Scenes

What is your job on the day of the show?

There is a lot to check on the day of the show. Sound and lighting technical checks are carried out. Dancers and other props need to be prepared. And, of course, we have to make sure that the contestants know their songs!

What happens if something goes wrong?

We try to soldier on! But sometimes it's impossible – that's the excitement of live shows. Diana's sickness last year is a good example – sometimes the contestant just needs to rest. We turn it into a story and work around it as best as we can.

When do contestants arrive on the day of the show?

The contestants arrive late morning. They are filed into the studio and rehearse right up until an hour before the show starts. They only get to rehearse their routines onstage twice, so the pressure on them to get it right is immense.

What happens in the run-up to a live show?

It's a long day! It lasts at least twelve hours. The audience is admitted to the studio about forty-five minutes before the show starts. The atmosphere in production gets a little frantic at this point! It's my role to double-check that everyone knows what he or she is supposed to be doing. There's a lot of pressure, but it's a really exciting job.

Saturday Schedule

1. **Contestants arrive and have breakfast.**

2. **Start make-up and hair.**

3. **Camera rehearsal on set.**

4. **Lunch.**

5. **Full dress rehearsal on set.**

6. **Meal break.**

7. **Audience admitted to studio.**

8. **Live show!**

What happens when a performance needs some special effects?

Most special effects are possible on *The X Factor*! Creating these effects is a highly specialised job with lots of health and safety issues. Whenever we are planning something extraordinary, we always have to complete a risk assessment. Lasers are quite problematic!

What's the biggest last-minute drama you've ever had?

I think that the scariest moment was when the insert tape arrived late from our post-production company – if it hadn't turned up, we wouldn't have had anything to show the audience about what the contestants had been doing in the week!↘

The stylists really enjoyed dressing Rhydian!

The skilled make-up artists work very hard to make sure that all the contestants look glamorous!

Everyone backstage was delighted
for Leon when he beat all the odds
and won *The X Factor*!

What is your role just before the live show starts?
I have to check the studio and make sure that the audience is in place. We don't want any gaps in the crowd, so I double-check that every seat is filled!

What do you do during the live show?
I watch the 'off air' feed with fingers crossed – if anything goes wrong it'll be my job to sort it out!

What happens during commercial breaks?
The warm-up man goes onstage and keeps the audience laughing and smiling. Meanwhile, the Judges and the crew have a short break – although the crew never leave their posts!

What's the most fun aspect of working backstage?
For me, it's got to be guessing who's going home each week! The backstage atmosphere is really electric during the live show. Everyone is excited and there really is a kind of magic in the air!

What happens after the show?
As soon as *The X Factor* is off air, *The Xtra Factor* takes over. The Judges usually leave pretty soon after the main show finishes, but the contestants often stay to chat to Holly Willoughby.

The Xtra Factor can sometimes be on air until after eleven o'clock, which doesn't leave much time for the contestants to change out of their 'on screen' outfits and say a quick hello to their families before heading to bed!

The crew is kept busy packing up equipment and making sure that the studio is left in good order, so they usually leave at about midnight. ↘

Same Difference were great fun!

Behind the Scenes

How many people work backstage?
There are approximately one hundred people working backstage on every live show of *The X Factor*!

Who are the floor crew?
The floor crew assist the contestants on the day of the live show. There is one floor manager and two or three assistants for every show.

There are between twelve and fourteen cameras recording each show. Some of them are fixed in position and some are held on a camera operator's shoulder. There are even some cameras high above the studio, so the camera operators have to climb rope ladders to reach them!

Path to Production
What was your career route?

PRODUCTION SECRETARY

↘

PRODUCTION CO-ORDINATOR

↘

LINE PRODUCER

What has been your most memorable moment while working on The X Factor?
It has to be the first incredible year of mass auditions in London. I could hardly believe my eyes when we turned up at six in the morning and saw thousands and thousands of people waiting in the rain!

Who was your favourite past contestant and why?
That's easy – Ray Quinn was definitely my favourite! He always had time for a smile and a chat, however much pressure he was feeling.

Who do you think has the X Factor?
For me, Leona Lewis stands out – I think she's fabulous!

The dressing rooms
are busy throughout
the live show!

Line Producer's Tip

Do you fancy working
behind the scenes? Whether
you want to be a camera
operator, producer or
director, the best start is to
become a runner. Get good
at making tea! You will get
to know everyone and you'll
develop a really good sense
of how the industry works.
After all, that's how Simon
Cowell got started!

The X Factor
FACTS

Check out these fascinating facts about your favourite show!

• The very first series of *The X Factor* began in September 2004.

• *The X Factor* is the biggest television talent competition in Europe!

• The most popular audition song choices for girls include 'Summertime', 'Somewhere Over the Rainbow', 'Hero' and 'How Do I Live Without You'.

• Leona Lewis scored a number one with her single 'A Moment Like This' and runner up Ray Quinn went to the top of the charts with his debut album.

• In *The Xtra Factor*, Dermot O'Leary and Holly Willoughby go head to head in Presentiators.

• Stylists get through as many as thirty cans of hairspray each day of filming!

• The British Prime Minister Gordon Brown is a fan of *The X Factor* and has even been known to write fan letters to contestants!

PREVIOUS WINNERS AND RUNNERS-UP

SERIES 1

Winner: **Steve Brookstein**
Runner-up: **G4**

SERIES 2

Winner: **Shayne Ward**
Runner-up: **Andy Abraham**

SERIES 3

Winner: **Leona Lewis**
Runner-up: **Ray Quinn**

SERIES 4

Winner: **Leon Jackson**
Runner-up: **Rhydian Roberts**

SERIES 5

Winner: **Alexandra Burke**
Runner-up: **JLS**

- The show is produced for ITV1 by FremantleMedia's talkbackTHAMES and Simon Cowell's production company SYCOtv.

- The most popular audition song choices for boys include 'Ain't No Sunshine', 'You Give Me Something', 'Yesterday' and 'I Believe I Can Fly'.

- A special celebrity edition of the show, called *The X Factor: Battle of the Stars*, featured nine stars including Lucy Benjamin, Chris Moyles and Paul Daniels.

- Alexandra Burke reached double Platinum status with her debut release 'Hallelujah'.

- Simon Cowell was recently ranked third on the Forbes 'TV Faces' list.

- *The X Factor* is rated as ITV's most popular programme while it airs.

- Four winners of *The X Factor* in a row have had the Christmas number-one single.

- *The X Factor* has been recognised by The BAFTAs (best entertainment show, two years running) and the National Television Awards (entertainment show of the year).

- Dannii Minogue has had a record-breaking eleven number-one club hits in the UK; more than any other female artist in the world.

- The MacDonald Brothers became a Scottish success story. They had a number-one hit in their home country as the first Scottish act signed by a Scottish label.

- *The X Factor* has travelled over 5,000 miles across Britain searching for the nation's best undiscovered talent.

- Grammy Award-winning popstar Paula Abdul has been a guest Judge on *The X Factor*.

- The official website (www.itv.com/xfactor) is the ultimate destination for fans of *The X Factor*, with all the latest videos, interviews with the Judges, behind the scenes footage and exit interviews.

- The format of *The X Factor* is shown in twentysix countries, including Denmark, Italy, Spain and India.

The X Factor QUIZ 1

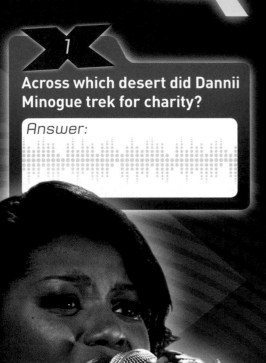

X 1
Across which desert did Dannii Minogue trek for charity?

Answer:

X 2
Who won series four?

Answer:

Here are some questions for all you avid fans, including details from previous series. Good luck!

X 3
Which Judge was ranked 3rd on the Forbes 'TV Faces' list?

Answer:

X 4
Which series final had 13.5 million viewers?

Answer:

Brenda Edwards

5

Which high-ranking politician is a fan of *The X Factor*?

Answer:

8

Who hosts *The X Factor*?

Answer:

11

Who won second place in series three?

Answer:

9

Who hosts *The Xtra Factor*?

Answer:

6

What was Simon Cowell's first job in the music industry?

Answer:

7

Name the four categories in *The X Factor*?

Answer:

10

Which football team does Dermot O'Leary support?

Answer:

Tabby

Answers:
1. Gobi Desert / 2. Leon Jackson / 3. Simon Cowell / 4. Series 5 / 5. Gordon Brown / 6. Post-boy / 7. Boys, girls, over 25s and groups / 8. Dermot O'Leary / 9. Holly Willoughby / 10. Arsenal / 11. Raymond Quinn

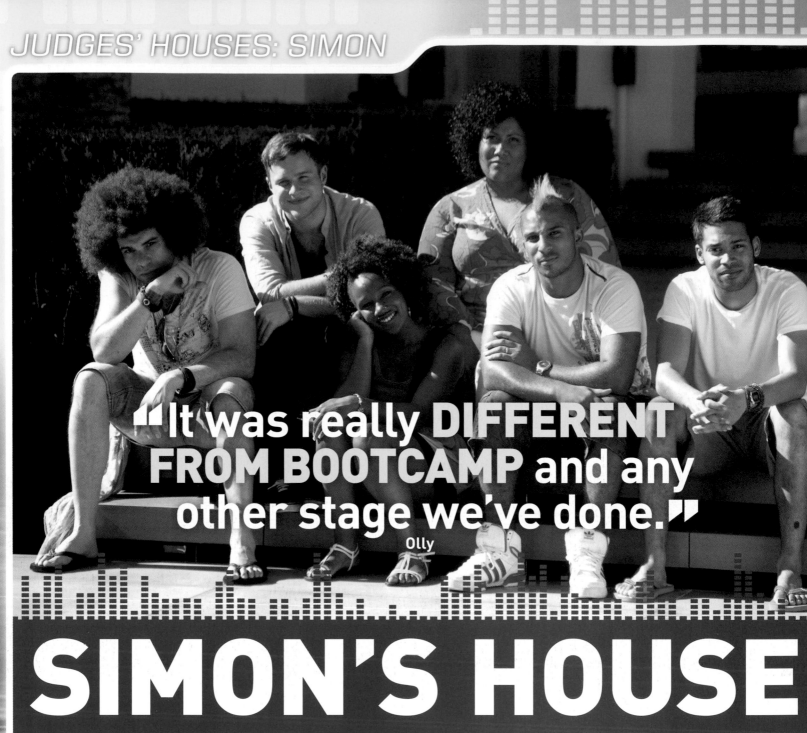

"It was really **DIFFERENT FROM BOOTCAMP** and any other stage we've done."
Olly

SIMON'S HOUSE

Fast Facts

Location:
Los Angeles

Category: Over 25's

Guest Mentor: Sinitta

Contestants:
Jaime Archer
Treyc Cohen
Danyl Johnson
Nicole Lawrence
Olly Murs
Daniel Pearce

 Simon took his acts to Los Angeles to soak up some of the superstar lifestyle as they competed to win a place in the live shows.

While visiting Simon's glamorous Los Angeles home, the Over 25s experienced a trip in a limo and spent time at the world-famous Beverly Wiltshire Hotel.

It was an intense, exciting time for the contestants, but they were also wracked with nerves. This was their last chance to prove to Simon that they had what it takes to make it all the way to the final.⌐

A rare moment of relaxation during the contestants' hectic schedule.

Profile

Name: Treyc Cohen
Age: 25
Home town: Birmingham
Job: Call centre worker
Audition city: Birmingham

Performing is hungry work!

Each act had to give two performances in front of Simon and Sinitta, with only basic accompaniment and very little practice. The pressure was immense, and for three of the six acts, this would be the end of the road . . .

"LA was **ABSOLUTELY AMAZING.**"
Olly

Simon treated his six acts like stars.

Profile

Name: Nicole Lawrence
Age: 31
Home town: Peterborough
Job: Care worker
Audition city: Birmingham

LOS ANGELES LOWDOWN

Los Angeles is the biggest city in the state of California. It is nicknamed the City of Angels, and it is the home of Hollywood. Many people call it the entertainment capital of the world, so it's no surprise that Simon made it his home!

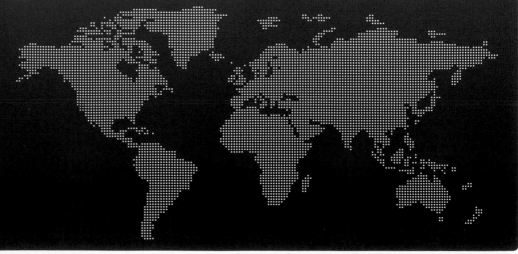

OVER 25S
SONG LIST

DANYL JOHNSON:
'Falling' and 'The First Time Ever I Saw Your Face'

OLLY MURS:
'Hang On In There Baby' and 'A Song For You'

JAMIE ARCHER:
'Stop Crying Your Heart Out' and 'Purple Rain'

DANIEL PEARCE:
'Praying for Time' and 'Have You Ever Really Loved a Woman'

NICOLA LAWRENCE:
'I Still Haven't Found What I'm Looking For' and 'Up to the Mountain'

TREYC COHEN:
'If You Love Me' and 'All the Man That I Need'

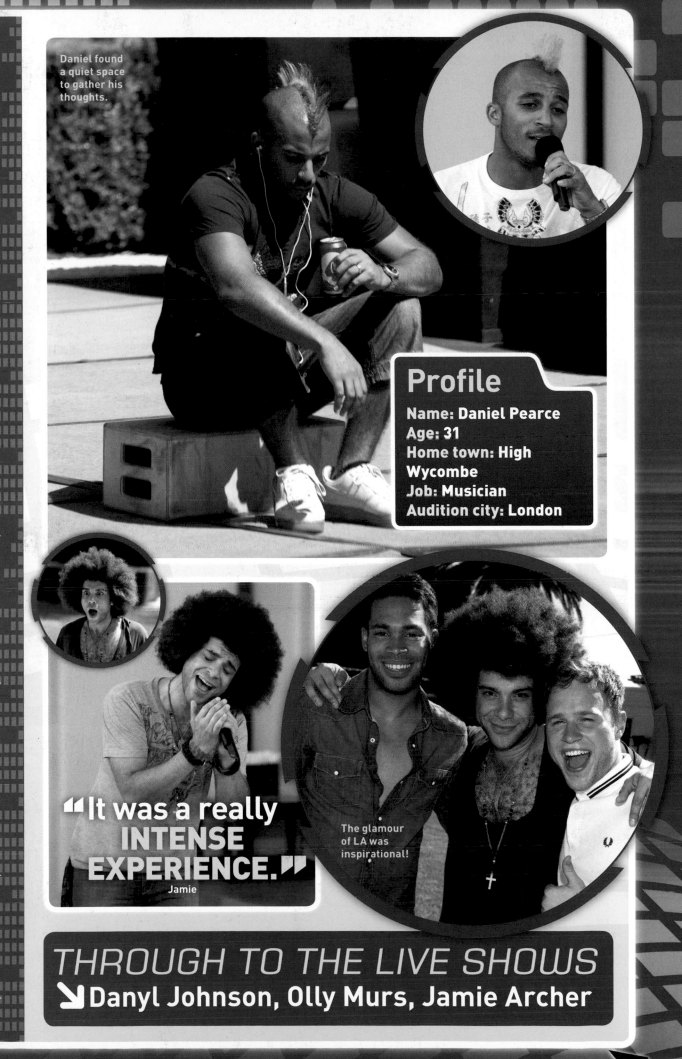

Daniel found a quiet space to gather his thoughts.

Profile
Name: Daniel Pearce
Age: 31
Home town: High Wycombe
Job: Musician
Audition city: London

"It was a really INTENSE EXPERIENCE."
Jamie

The glamour of LA was inspirational!

THROUGH TO THE LIVE SHOWS
↘ Danyl Johnson, Olly Murs, Jamie Archer

CHERYL'S HOUSE

Fast Facts

Location: Marrakech

Category: Boys

Guest Mentor: Will Young

Contestants:
Daniel Fox
Duane Lamonte
Ethan Boroian
Joseph McElderry
Lloyd Daniels
Rikki Loney

 Cheryl jetted off to Marrakech with her six acts, hoping to instil some Moroccan magic in their performances!

The contestants loved Marrakech, but they could not forget the reason why they were there. For these six boys, everything depended on the next few days. They had bonded during Bootcamp and had shared many challenging experiences, but now they were battling for three places, and three of them would go home with their dreams in tatters. ↘

There was time for a bit of fun alongside the pressures of performing!

"NERVES TOOK OVER most of the feelings most of the time.**"**
Joseph

Profile

Name: Daniel Fox
Age: 18
Home town: Manchester
Job: Unemployed
Audition city: Manchester

The boys enjoyed the sunshine of Marrakech.

Rikki put his heart and soul into his songs.

Cheryl asked Will Young to help her choose the three acts that had the best chance of winning The X Factor. Will's experience of winning a TV talent competition helped him to see who would shine and who would crumble under the pressure of live shows.

As they stood in front of Cheryl and Will, each boy knew that this was one of the most important moments of his life. Each performance they gave had to be emotional, controlled, powerful and persuasive. Who would exceed expectations... and who would fall by the wayside? ☺

"It was a
FANTASTIC EXPERIENCE."
Joseph

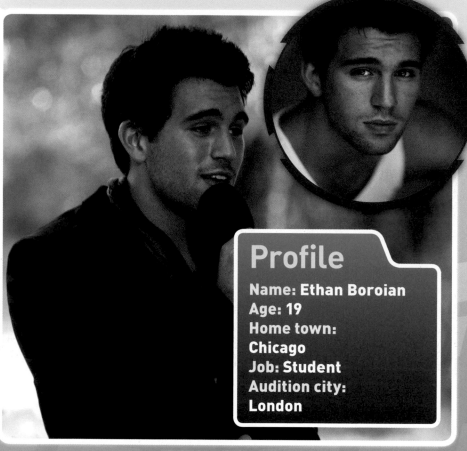

Profile

Name: Ethan Boroian
Age: 19
Home town:
Chicago
Job: Student
Audition city:
London

MAGICAL
MARRAKECH

↘ Marrakech is known as the Red City, and it is the home of the largest traditional market in Morocco. The city also has one of the busiest squares in the world, Djemaa el Fna. This square is alive with colour and sound, and is always buzzing with storytellers, acrobats, dancers and musicians. At night, the square is filled with food stalls and becomes a massive open-air restaurant!

BOYS SONG LIST

ETHAN BOROIAN
'Chasing Pavements' and 'I Guess That's Why They Call It the Blues'

LLOYD DANIELS
'She's The One' and 'I'm Yours'

JOSEPH MCELDERRY
'Imagine' and 'Sorry Seems to be the Hardest Word'

RIKKI LONEY
'I Get the Sweetest Feeling' and 'You've Got a Friend'

DANIEL FOX
'Already There' and 'Without You'

DUANE LAMONTE
'Back to Black' and 'Closer'

This is the most nerve-wracking moment of the contestants' lives.

Profile
Name: Duane Lamonte
Age: 24
Home town: London
Job: Youth worker
Audition city: London

The boys were all keen to impress their mentor.

"Marrakech was **ABSOLUTELY AMAZING.**"
Lloyd

THROUGH TO THE LIVE SHOWS
↘ Joseph McElderry, Lloyd Daniels, Rikki Loney

"**We got to SWIM with DOLPHINS!**"
Stacey

DANNII'S HOUSE

Fast Facts

Location:
Dubai

Category: Girls

Guest Mentor: Kylie Minogue

Contestants:
Nicole Jackson
Stacey McClean
Rachel Adedeji
Lucie Jones
Stacey Soloman
Despina Pilavakis

 Dannii chose uber-cool Dubai as the place to put her final six acts through their paces.

While staying in Dubai, Dannii lined up several wonderful surprises for her group. The girls went swimming with dolphins and also enjoyed a private meal with their mentor, to which the cameras were not invited!

As well as enjoying the delights of Dubai, the contestants had work to do. All their hopes and dreams were riding on how they handled the pressure of this stage. They had to persuade Dannii to put them through to the live shows.↘

The girls formed a close bond.

Stacey was thrilled by the glamour of Dubai!

Profile

Name: Nicole Jackson
Age: 18
Home town: Bristol
Job: Bar worker
Audition city: Cardiff

"We didn't expect to go somewhere like DUBAI. It was just ABSOLUTELY STUNNING."

Lucie

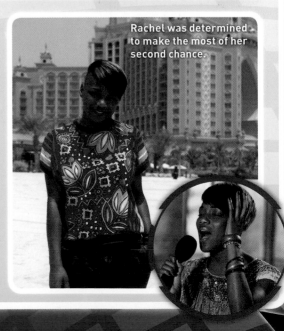

Rachel was determined to make the most of her second chance.

Dannii enlisted the help of her superstar sister to decide which three acts should win the coveted places. With their future depending on two last performances, the girls were equally excited and terrified. Who would have the opportunity to become a star . . . and who would be going home? . . .⊗

"Dubai was AMAZING!"
Stacey

No one wanted to lose their chance of stardom.

Profile

Name: Stacey McClean
Age: 20
Home town: Blackpool
Job: Office worker
Audition city: London

DUBAI DATA

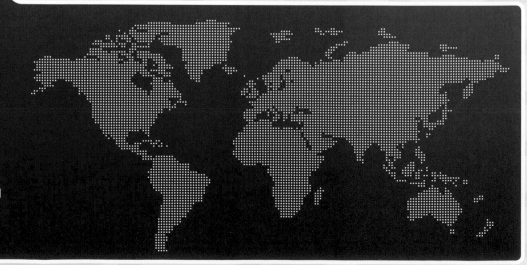

➜ The state of Dubai is located on the coast of the Persian Gulf, and its name has become inextricably linked with wealth, glamour and beauty – the perfect setting for Dannii and the Girls group.

GIRLS SONG LIST

DESPINA PILAVAKIS:
'All By Myself' and 'The Voice Within'

LUCIE JONES:
'If I Were a Boy' and 'Anything For You'

NICOLE JACKSON:
'Lately'

RACHEL ADEDEJI:
'I Still Haven't Found What I'm Looking For' and 'Nobody Knows'

STACEY McCLEAN:
'Sometimes' and 'Nothing Compares 2U'

STACEY SOLOMAN:
'Somewhere Over the Rainbow' and 'Think Twice'

Profile
Name: Despina Pilavakis
Age: 20
Home town: London
Job: Music student
Audition city: Manchester

It's a long way from a sleepy village in Wales to a glamorous hotel in Dubai!

The successful girls could hardly believe that they had made it to the live shows.

THROUGH TO THE LIVE SHOWS
↘ Lucie Jones, Rachel Adedeji, Stacey Soloman

❝The whole experience was MENTALLY DRAINING, but it was exciting as well.❞
Kandy Rain

LOUIS'S HOUSE

Fast Facts

Location:
Lake Como

Category: Groups

Guest Mentor: Ronan Keating

Contestants:
De-Tour
Harmony Hood
John and Edward Grimes
Kandy Rain
Miss F.R.A.N.K.
Project A

 Louis chose tranquil Lake Como as the setting for the groups' last chance to win a place in the live shows.

The groups were tense and excited when they arrived at Lake Como. They could hardly believe that they had made it this far in the competition – it all seemed like a delightful dream!

However, things were about to get very real. Only half of them would be able to continue their journey towards the final. For the others, the dream would become a nightmare.↘

Hopes were high as the groups prepared to perform their first songs in front of Louis and Ronan.

Profile

Name: Project A
Age: 19–25
Home town: Leeds
Job: Cheerleaders
Audition city: Manchester

All the contestants practised hard.

Louis's six acts were all courageous, ambitious and talented. They had battled their way through the auditions and Bootcamp. It was impossible to know which of them would have the strength and determination to make it through this last stage.

"Lake Como was very tranquil. It was like A FAIRYTALE."
Kandy Rain

Everyone was excited by the opportunity that beckoned!

Profile

Name: De-Tour
Age: 20 and 21
Home town: Liverpool
Job: Singers
Audition city: Manchester

Unlike the other categories, the groups had to rely on others to stay strong too. If one person faltered, they would not only be letting themselves down; they would be destroying the dreams of their friends as well.

CALM
LAKE COMO

↘ Lake Como is one of the most famous Italian lakes . . . and one of the most beautiful. It is popular with tourists for sailing, windsurfing and kitesurfing, and the weather is usually mild. The lake is edged with beautiful villas, and it was the ideal place for Louis's nervous groups to relax and give their best performances.

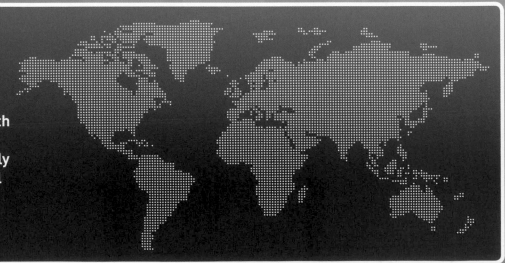

GROUPS' SONG LIST

PROJECT A:
'What's Up' and 'Pokerface'

HARMONY HOOD:
'Where is the Love' and 'Never Can Say Goodbye''

MISS F.R.A.N.K.:
'Respect' and 'Cry Me a River'

JOHN AND EDWARD:
'I Want It That Way' and 'When Will I Be Famous'

KANDY RAIN:
'I Kissed a Girl' and 'Paparazzi'

DE-TOUR:
'Till There Was You' and 'Tiny Dancer'

Profile
Name: Harmony Hood
Age: 18–23
Home town: Coventry
Job: Singers
Audition city: Birmingham

Louis invited Ronan Keating to assist him in judging the quality of the groups and deciding who should be given the chance of a lifetime. Together, Louis and Ronan watched each group perform two songs. A difficult choice lay in front of them. Which groups had done enough to take them to the live shows? ✪

THROUGH TO THE LIVE SHOWS

➘ **Miss F.R.A.N.K.**

➘ **John and Edward Grimes**

➘ **Kandy Rain**

The X Factor
QUIZ 2

Well done! You have made it through to the next round. How many questions do you think you can answer this time?

X 1
What is the name of Cheryl Cole's band?

Answer:

X 2
In what year did *The X Factor* begin?

Answer:

X 3
Who was the winner of series two?

Answer:

X 4
Which show gives watchers all the backstage gossip?

Answer:

X 5
What is the nationality of The MacDonald Brothers?

Answer:

Rhydian

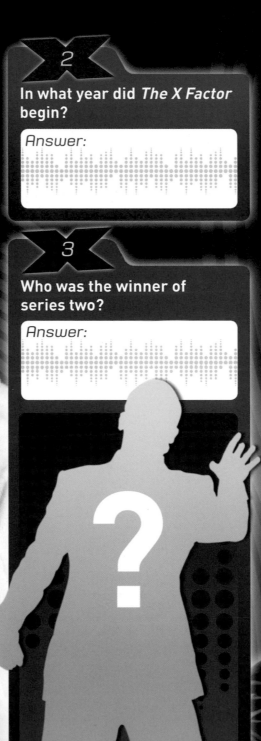

The MacDonald Brothers

Rachel Hylton

8
Who came second in series five?

Answer:

9
Which bin-man was runner-up in series two?

Answer:

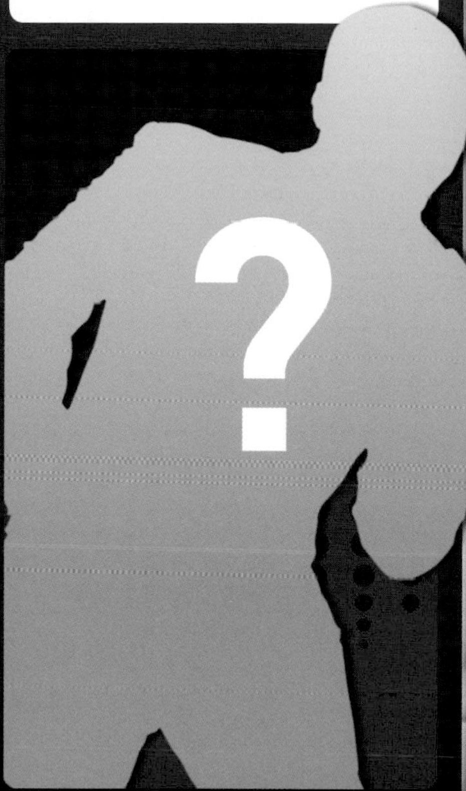

11
Which Judge has more number-one club hits in the UK than any other female artist?

Answer:

6
In which country did Louis Walsh grow up?

Answer:

7
What is the prize for winning *The X Factor*?

Answer:

10
What was the name of Leona Lewis's first single?

Answer:

Leona Lewis

Answers:
1. Girls Aloud / 2. 2004 / 3. Shayne Ward / 4. The Xtra Factor / 5. Scottish / 6. Ireland /
7. A recording contract / 8. JLS / 9. Andy Abraham / 10. A Moment Like This / 11. Dannii Minogue

BOOTCAMP

The lucky few who have made it through the auditions now face their hardest challenge yet. There is no room for error: one mistake could cost these hopefuls their dream! As nerves jangle and the tension skyrockets, the Judges head for Bootcamp...

Bootcamp was held at the famous Hammersmith Apollo, but even before they stepped onstage, the pressure increased to boiling point. As the contestants arrived in their hotel the evening before the first day, they faced a daunting challenge. They had to organise themselves into small groups, pick a song from a list

Christina Pittaway

Daniel Pearce

Jamie Archer

the Judges gave them, and prepare a performance that would keep them in the competition. For the acts performing the following day, this meant that they had less than twenty-four hours to prepare. The heat was on!

"Bootcamp will MAKE OR BREAK them."
Dannii

Project A

The following day saw the start of a terrifying process for the acts competing to win a place in the live shows. After a sleepless night, half of the acts faced the Judges while the other half filled the front seats and became the audience. ↘

Rachel Adedeji

Daniel Fox

Lucie Jones

Despina Pilavakis

Although the acts were performing onstage together, the Judges were still assessing them individually. It was important for each act to concentrate only on his or her own performance.

Bootcamp was exhausting, demanding and unnerving for the anxious contestants. They were stressed, sleep deprived and

Duane Lamonte

Danyl Johnson

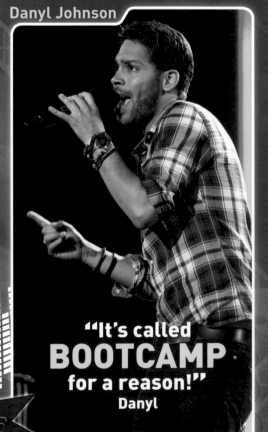

"It's called **BOOTCAMP** for a reason!"
Danyl

worried, and sometimes it was only their adrenaline that got them through the day!

Not everyone can cope with the pressures of Bootcamp. Daryl Markham's Bootcamp partner walked out, saying that he couldn't handle it any more.

One of the members of girl band Miss Fitz didn't even turn up to Bootcamp, and the remaining girls were forced to become a duo at the last minute!

When they were put into groups, Ethan Boroian, Danyl Johnson and Rikki Loney banded together

John & Edward Grimes

and chose to sing Katie Perry's 'Hot and Cold'. They decided to give it an alternative treatment, but it went horrifically wrong! Luckily for the three boys, the Judges remembered their brilliant first auditions and gave them another chance. ↘

Nicole Jackson

Rikki Loney

Lewis Clay

Ethan Boroain

Through to Judges' Houses

Under 25 Girls
Mentor: Dannii
Group:
Lucie Jones
Nicole Jackson
Rachel Adedeji
Stacey McClean
Despina Pilavakis
Stacey Soloman

Bootcamp Schedule

8.30am: Session 1

10.30am: Judges' break

11am: Session 2

1pm: Judges' dinner

2pm: Session 3

4pm: Judges' break

4.30pm: Session 4

6.30pm: End of day

For some contestants, Bootcamp changed their plans completely. Three girls partnered up on the first day and gave such a phenomenal performance that Simon suggested they should form a group. That's how Miss F.R.A.N.K. was born!

It's tough for the Judges as well as for the contestants.

They have to stay alert throughout a gruelling schedule, because one wrong decision could mean that they miss out on a future superstar!

The Judges spend their Bootcamp days making and breaking dreams. They have to try to be fair and consistent with their marking, but personality is bound to come into it!

At the end of Bootcamp, it was the Judges' unenviable task to whittle all the magnificent performers down to just twenty-four. It was a tough job, but they had to do it, and at last they were able to tell the lucky ones that they were going on to the next stage of the competition.

Stacey McClean

"We've got some **GREAT PEOPLE** – better than any other year."
Louis

Nicole Lawrence

At last it was time for the Judges to find out which category each of them had been allocated. Now it was their turn to have to wait to find out the results! After a few nail-biting moments, the categories were allocated. The Judges were buzzing with excitement!

The fortunate twenty-four could hardly believe they had made it. After days of Bootcamp pressure, it seemed like a dream! But even as they went crazy with excitement, a new realisation was dawning. Bootcamp might have seemed tough, but it was nothing compared to the next stage... ↘

Stacey Soloman

Jaz Ellington

Treyc Cohen

Through to Judges' Houses

Over 25s
Mentor: Simon
Group:
Daniel Pearce
Danyl Johnson
Olly Murs
James Archer
Nicole Lawrence
Treyc Cohen

Kandy Rain

Faye Bray

Bootcamp's Best

Miss F.R.A.N.K. gave a phenomenal performance of 'That's Life'. They blew everyone away when they turned an old classic into a modern-sounding song with a hip urban flavour.

Through to Judges' Houses

Groups
Mentor: Louis
Group:
De-Tour
Frank
John and Edward Grimes
Kandy Rain
Project A
Harmony Hood

Paul Keogh

Princess Sweetie

Joseph McElderry

"I FORGOT THE WORDS, but I'm hoping that the Judges didn't notice!"
Joe

Olly Murs

Lloyd Daniels

Harmony Hood

 Final Twelve's Bootcamp Song List:

Danyl Johnson
'Hot and Cold' &
'Holding Back the Years'

James Archer
'One' & 'With or Without You'

Olly Murs
'One' & 'Your Song'

Joseph McElderry
'Use Somebody' &
'Praying for Time'

Lloyd Daniels
'Apologise' &
'You Are Not Alone'

Rikki Loney
'Hot and Cold' & 'Last Request'

John and Edward
'Apologise' & 'You Are Not Alone'

Kandy Rain
'Apologise' &
'Stop Crying Your Heart Out'

Miss F.R.A.N.K.
'That's Life' &
'Wishing On a Star'

Stacey Soloman
'Use Somebody' & 'There'll You'll Be'

Lucie Jones
'Hero' & 'Hurt'

Rachel Adedeji
'Ain't No Mountain' & 'Last Request'

The X Factor QUIZ 3

1

On what TV show was Cheryl Cole first discovered?

Answer:

2

In series five, who went down with laryngitis in week five?

Answer:

Congratulations! You have made it through to the final round, but do you have what it takes to win?

3

Who was the runner-up of series one?

Answer:

4

How many yesses must a contestant receive to make it through to Bootcamp?

Answer:

Chico Slimani

5
What BAFTA did *The X Factor* win two years in a row?

Answer:

8
Which companies produce *The X Factor*?

Answer:

11
Which Judge once starred in *Home and Away*?

Answer:

9
Which Judge was the winning mentor of *The X Factor* 2008?

Answer:

6
How many series' of *The X Factor* have there been so far?

Answer:

7
Which celebrities compete in *The Xtra Factor's* Presentiators?

Answer:

10
How old was Holly Willoughby when she was spotted by a modelling agency?

Answer:

Answers:
1. *Popstars: The Rivals* / 2. Diana Vickers / 3. G4 / 4. *Three* / 5. *Best Entertainment Show* / 6. *Six* / 7. Dermot O'Leary and Holly Willoughby / 8. FremantleMedia's talkbackTHAMES and SYCOtv / 9. Cheryl Cole / 10. *Fourteen* / 11. Dannii Minogue

Nikitta Angus

73

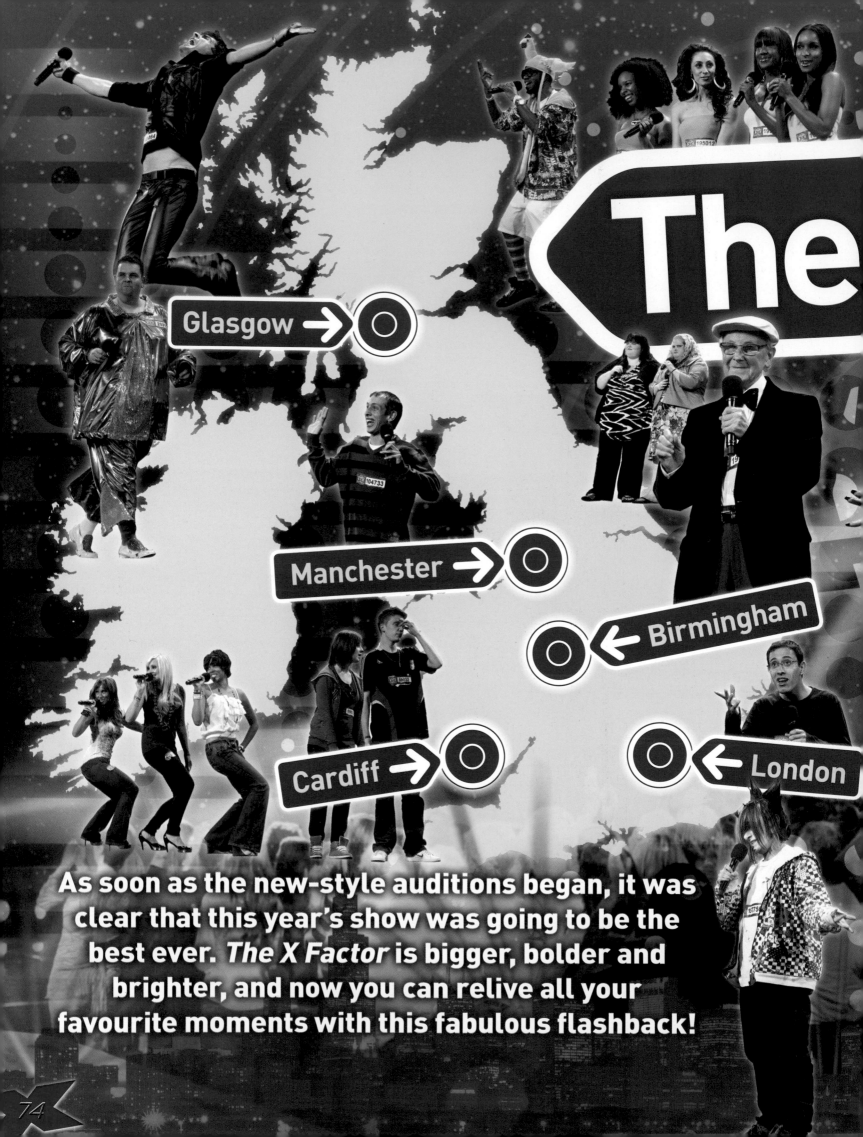

Glasgow →◎

The

Manchester →◎

◎← Birmingham

Cardiff →◎

◎← London

As soon as the new-style auditions began, it was clear that this year's show was going to be the best ever. *The X Factor* is bigger, bolder and brighter, and now you can relive all your favourite moments with this fabulous flashback!

AUDITIONS

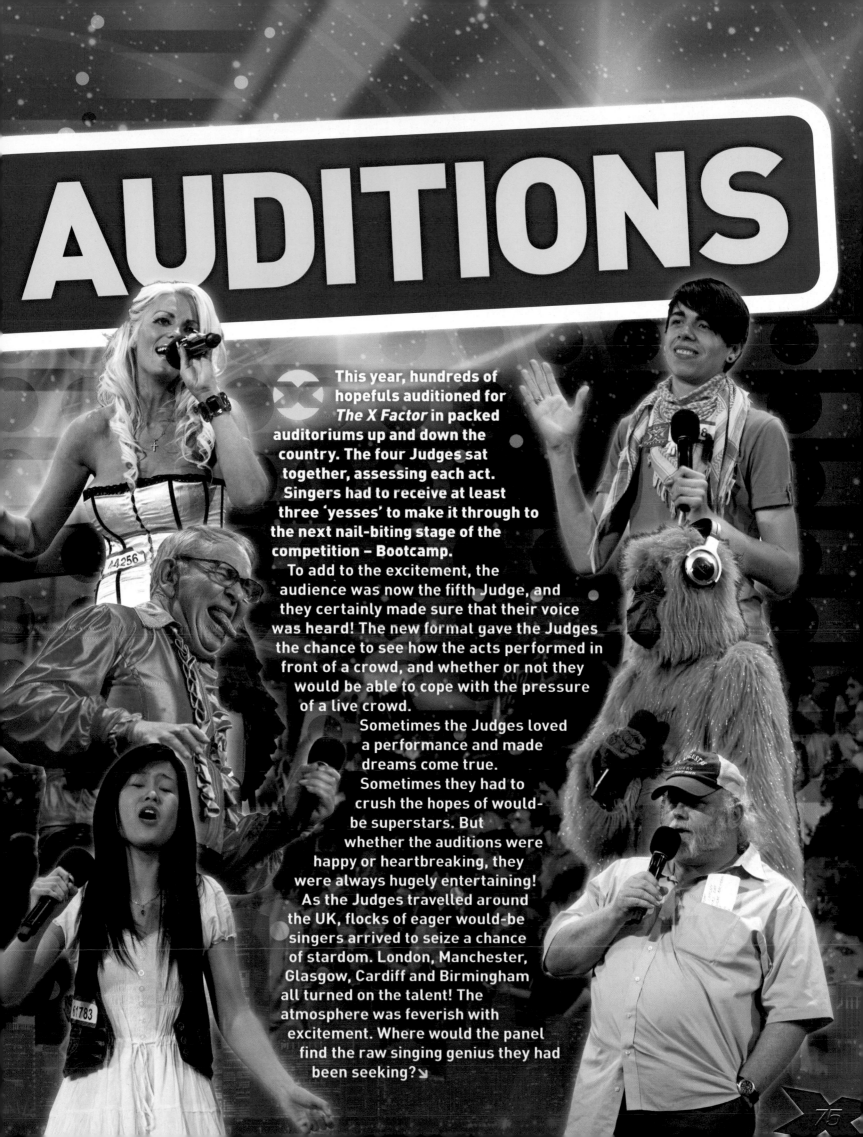

This year, hundreds of hopefuls auditioned for *The X Factor* in packed auditoriums up and down the country. The four Judges sat together, assessing each act. Singers had to receive at least three 'yesses' to make it through to the next nail-biting stage of the competition – Bootcamp.

To add to the excitement, the audience was now the fifth Judge, and they certainly made sure that their voice was heard! The new format gave the Judges the chance to see how the acts performed in front of a crowd, and whether or not they would be able to cope with the pressure of a live crowd.

Sometimes the Judges loved a performance and made dreams come true. Sometimes they had to crush the hopes of would-be superstars. But whether the auditions were happy or heartbreaking, they were always hugely entertaining! As the Judges travelled around the UK, flocks of eager would-be singers arrived to seize a chance of stardom. London, Manchester, Glasgow, Cardiff and Birmingham all turned on the talent! The atmosphere was feverish with excitement. Where would the panel find the raw singing genius they had been seeking?↘

"**A MILLION** per cent yes!"
Louis

"**We're going to need people with CLOCKS!**"
Simon

The Stunners

— ✗ —

Episode: 2
The Stunners certainly stunned the Judges . . . for all the wrong reasons!

"You didn't sing a single NOTE in tune!"

Simon

Demi Cullum

— ✗ —

Episode: 4
Bubbly student Demi Cullum dreams of being a superstar, but nerves got the better of her at her audition.

"You are just ADORABLE!"

Dannii

Ian

Ian Russell went one step further than most hopefuls – he dressed up as his idol! Ian hoped that his enthusiasm and sense of style would persuade the Judges to put him through to Bootcamp. Just in case they needed convincing, his rucksack was stuffed with alternative costumes to match all the songs he could sing. How could he fail to impress? Sadly, Simon wasn't swayed by the Guy With Style. "The outfit's awful, the song's dreadful; it's absolutely bottom of the list in any horrible cabaret show," he said.

Sister Act

✗

Episode: 1
Sisters Emma and Samantha were determined to keep trying – even though they were evicted for singing in the street!

"**Arguably TWICE as bad as before!**"

Simon

"**You've got a full house – FOUR YESSES!**"

Simon

Katy Bullock

✗

Episode: 1
The Judges loved Katy Bullock's biker chic!

Allan Busby

Episode: 3
Allan Busby has dreamed of being an entertainer since the age of ten. The Judges said no – but the audience loved him!

"I've NEVER seen a rhythm like it!"
Cheryl

Joseph McElderry

Episode: 1
Joe's incredible voice got a standing ovation.

"Big, big, big YES!"
Cheryl

103331

104733

Ashwin

Hot-tempered Ashwin returned to *The X Factor* after failing his audition in 2008. He was still determined to achieve his dream of pop stardom! Over the year he has built up a fanbase called the Ashwinites. "I believe I'm ready to take the world by storm!" he declared. The audience cheered and whistled as Ashwin sang 'Spirit in the Sky', but Simon was rolling his eyes. "Now's the time to have a wake-up call in your life," he said. The Judges didn't think Ashwin could win *The X Factor*, and he had to leave without a pass to Bootcamp. But he was happy that he had done the Ashwinites proud!

Ashanti Webbe

Episode: 3
Ashanti Webbe was very nervous, but there was no need for her to worry. She sailed through to the next round!

2 Gorgeous 4 Words

Episode: 3
2 Gorgeous 4 Words left the Judges speechless.

"Absolutely YES!"

Louis

"EVERYTHING! was wrong!"

Simon

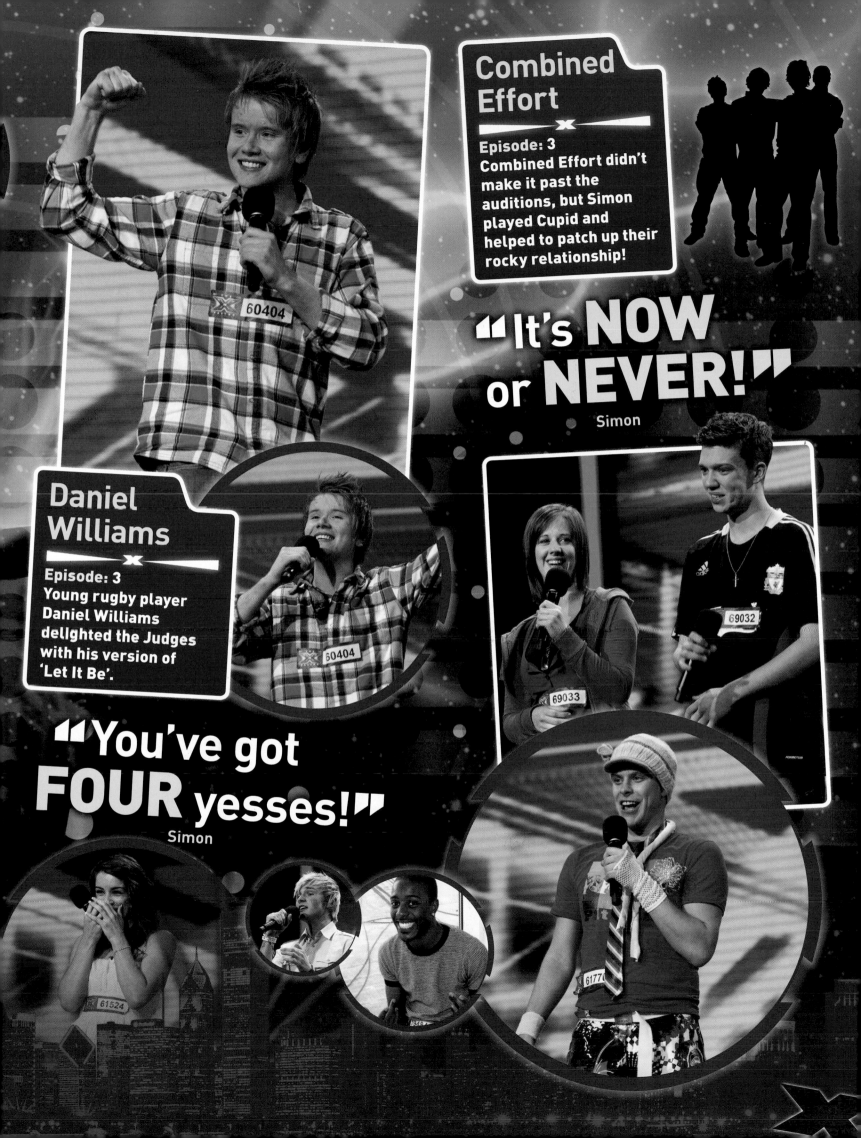

Combined Effort

Episode: 3
Combined Effort didn't make it past the auditions, but Simon played Cupid and helped to patch up their rocky relationship!

"It's NOW or NEVER!"
Simon

Daniel Williams

Episode: 3
Young rugby player Daniel Williams delighted the Judges with his version of 'Let It Be'.

"You've got FOUR yesses!"
Simon

Nathan Leslie
×

Episode: 1
Nathan Leslie hoped that the chicken on his head would distract the judges from his singing.

"You can't SING!"
Simon

"For me, it's easy... it's a YES!"
Dannii

Miss Fitz
×

Episode: 2
Miss Fitz' sensational arrangement of 'Toxic' delighted the audience and the Judges!

Steve
Steve Loczy is a payroll clerk by day, but inside him is a cowboy waiting to burst free. His Wild West swagger, Stetson, rattlesnake cowboy boots and fringed shirt were all in place . . . but his singing was ropier than a rodeo!

Behrouz Ghaemi

x

Episode: 2
Behrouz Ghaemi was brimming with confidence, convinced that he had the X Factor. The Judges agreed that he was hugely entertaining!

"There is something intriguingly CRAZY about you!"
Cheryl

Fouad Djaoublia

x

Episode: 3
Fouad Djaoublia's dreams of a career in music were shattered when the Judges said no, but he was delighted by the warm response he had from the audience!

"This was like something out of STAR WARS!"
Simon

Hubba

Episode: 4
Hubba's shiny outfit and yellow shoes brightened up the stage but didn't impress the Judges.

"It is a resounding NO!"
Simon

Kyle Campbell

Episode: 1
Scotland's biggest Girls Aloud fan impressed Cheryl, but the other Judges weren't convinced.

"Simply for the back chat, it's a YES!"
Cheryl

Ron

Ron Daniel's cutting-edge hairstyle wowed the Judges and amazed the audience. He insists that his locks don't make it difficult for him to see, but he has to get up at half-past three every morning to get his hair ready!
Ron sang his own song at his audition, but the Judges didn't like it. "It's different but it's not right," said Louis.

Carla Schettini

x

Episode: 4
Carla Schettini presented Louis with a tie made of his clan tartan, but it wasn't enough to get her through to Bootcamp!

"Louis got a **TIE!**"
Simon

Diana and Jazz

x

Episode: 4
Diana's singing partner Jazz got stage fright and couldn't sing a note!

"I'd be happy if the dog even **BARKED!**"
Louis

"That was a RACKET wasn't it!"
Simon

"STICK to the modelling, girls."
Simon

Duane Lamonte

Episode: 1
Duane Lamonte made it through to Bootcamp last year, and hoped that this year he could do even better.

Eileen Chapman

Episode: 5/6
Eileen has loved singing all her life; she can remember practising in the air-raid shelter as a little girl! She dreams of making a record, and she certainly won Simon's heart.

"You made an old lady very, HAPPY."

Eileen

"Love you this year...YES!"

Cheryl

Blue Gorilla

—✗—

Episode: 1
Simon was not in the mood for a blue gorilla.

Danyl Johnson

—✗—

Episode: 1
Danyl's electrifying audition got a standing ovation from Simon.

> "The **PERFECT** audition!"
>
> Dannii

> "I don't want to do this **ANY MORE!**"
>
> Simon

Tom

Tom Idelson arrived at the auditions with a great attitude . . . and an unusual singing voice. His philosophy is that everyone has something unique that makes them stand out, and he hoped that his love of music could win him a place on The X Factor!

However, Tom's high-pitched version of a Tom Jones classic didn't impress the Judges. When he did the splits onstage, Cheryl's eyes nearly popped out of her head! "That's not what I'm looking for," said Simon.

Jade Fubara

Episode: 3
Schoolgirl Jade Fubara stood out from the crowd with her raw, amazing talent.

"It's NOW or NEVER!"
Simon

Jamie Archer

Episode: 2
Jamie Archer's burning passion for music set the stage on fire and had Simon singing along!

"You've got FOUR yesses!"
Simon

Shanna Goodhead
✗
Episode: 4
Shanna's dreams of changing life for herself and her family took a big leap forward when she made it through to Bootcamp!

"You have a REALLY natural, raw talent!"
Cheryl

William Hooper
✗
Episode: 4
Everyone enjoyed William Hooper's smooth style – even Simon was clicking his fingers!

"You're a BORN ENTERTAINER!"
Louis

Aaron

Aaron arrived at his audition feeling full of confidence about his unique singing voice. He breezed on to the stage and launched into his song. He swayed his hips, danced and sang as the Judges looked on in amazement. His legs moved as if they were made of rubber!
"Ten out of ten for trying," said Cheryl. Simon agreed. "That doesn't mean you're going through to the next round," he said, "but effort . . . great." Aaron was happy with that!

It Takesz 2

Episode: 5/6
Russell and Katie have been together for four years and work as entertainers. They were determined to seize their chance to win over the Judges!

> "You guys are really **SWEET** together"
> Dannii

Gisela Lee

Episode: 4
Gisela Lee's pout didn't cut any ice with the Judges!

> "You **CAN'T** use jetlag as an excuse!"
> Simon

Maurice Siegel
×
Episode: 5/6
Maurice Siegel has over 500 fans in Southend... but sadly the Judges are not among them!

Dominic Harris
×
Episode: 5/6
Dominic Harris made it all the way to the Judges' Houses stage two years ago, but his nerves got the better of him and he fell apart at his last audition. This time he was determined to show the Judges that he had his nerves under control!

"I got scared when the TONGUE came out!"
Dannii

"You are really, REALLY GOOD!"
Simon

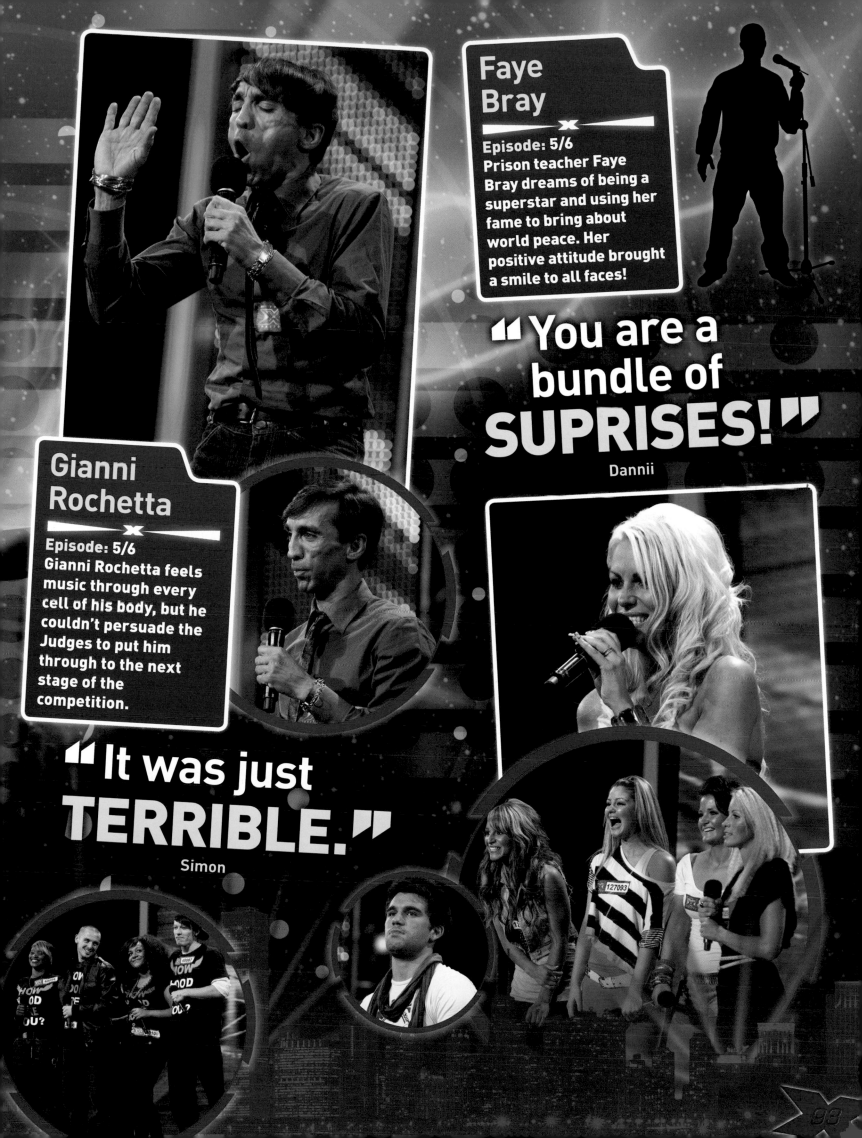

Faye Bray

x

Episode: 5/6
Prison teacher Faye Bray dreams of being a superstar and using her fame to bring about world peace. Her positive attitude brought a smile to all faces!

"**You are a bundle of SUPRISES!**"
Dannii

Gianni Rochetta

x

Episode: 5/6
Gianni Rochetta feels music through every cell of his body, but he couldn't persuade the Judges to put him through to the next stage of the competition.

"**It was just TERRIBLE.**"
Simon

X FINDING THE FACTOR

The X Factor isn't **just** about finding singing talent. A true star has something more – a quality that sets them apart from the others in the competition. Part of that is the unique look you create for yourself!

Your individual sense of style is a huge part of what makes you special. Before you audition for the Judges, think about all the elements that make you unique. Make sure that your hair, make-up and clothes truly reflect the real you!

"You STAND OUT from the crowd!"
Louis

Kandy Rain

Stacey McClean

Jamie Archer

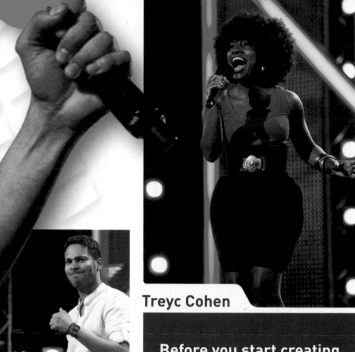

Treyc Cohen

Danyl Johnson

Daniel Pearce

Before you start creating an image for yourself, you need to think about what sort of person you are. Your look should reflect your personality. Ask yourself these questions to kick-start your creativity!

What sort of music do you sing?

How would you describe your natural style?

Who is your pop idol?

What are your favourite colours?

What are your favourite fabrics?

Do you wear jewellery?

What three words would you use to describe yourself?

"You tick ALL the boxes!"
Louis

Lucie Jones

Duane Lamonte

The most important thing is to keep your own individual sense of style. The Judges will love to see that you are happy with yourself. Confidence is one of the most important tools you have!

Miss Frank

John & Edward Grimes

Make-up

Creating the perfect look for your audition is super-important, because first impressions count! Check out these top tips to create total on-stage glamour.

Stacey McClean

"SUPERSTARS being created!"
Dannii

MAKE-UP DOS AND DON'TS

DO think about your best features and use make-up to accentuate them.
DON'T plaster make-up on – let your natural beauty shine through.
DO work out a skincare regime.
DON'T use out-of-date make-up products.
DO remove make-up before you go to bed.
DON'T try to hide behind extreme make-up – the Judges will see through that!
DO find out what kind of skin you have and use colours that suit you.
DON'T worry about blemishes – that's what concealer is for!
DO check your face in a mirror before you walk on stage.

Project A

SMOOTH CANVAS

Your skin is your canvas, so you need to take care of it! For flawless skin, make sure that you drink plenty of water, eat fruit and vegetables, and always protect your skin against the sun.

1. Clean and moisturise your skin.
2. Apply a light foundation all over your face, and blend it down onto your neck.
3. Lightly dust a little loose powder over your face and neck to give your foundation staying power.
4. Use a neutral blush under your cheek bone, and blend it into your skin with an upwards motion.
5. Dust bronzing powder over your cheeks with a big, soft brush.

ucie Jones

STRIKING EYES

The eyes are the windows of the soul, so you need to express yourself through them. For natural chic, simply add a layer of black mascara. But for show-stopping eyes, full of smouldering impact, you need to get dramatic!

1. Draw around each eye with a black eyeliner, staying close to the lash line.
2. Use a small brush to blend dark brown eyeshadow at the outside corner of each eye. Brush a medium brown eyeshadow into the crease of each eyelid to define your socket line. Finally, use a highlighting shade at the inside corner of each eye.
3. Add a coat of mascara to add volume and length.

Iiss Frank

BEAUTY TIP
Take your cosmetics bag to the audition with you – you may need to refresh your make-up before you sing.

LOVELY LIPS

Whether you prefer the natural look or head-turning red lips, you need to think about your pout. Attention will be on your mouth when you sing, so keep your lips soft and moisturised. For the natural look, just add a little clear lip gloss.

1. Apply lip liner all over your lips.
2. Using a lip brush, apply a layer of lipstick. Keep adding layers until you have the look you want.
3. Use a sparkling lip gloss for added glamour!

AUDITION TIP
Smile! Smiling puts you in a great frame of mind and shows that you are confident, friendly and warm.

Rachel Adedeji

Fashion

Looking cool and confident in your clothes is an art. You have to discover your own unique style. Find clothes that make you look and feel fantastic, and your confidence will shine out!

"I'm CONFIDENT NOW and believe in myself!"

Rikki

33

FASHION DOS AND DON'TS
DO wear clothes that match your singing style and personality.
DON'T wear clothes that are too small or too big for you. The best fit is not too tight and not too loose. You should wear the clothes – don't let the clothes wear you!
DO think about your accessories. These are the details of your look. You will show the Judges that you are capable of focusing on every detail to achieve perfection!
DON'T wear white socks!
DO research magazines for the latest trends.
DON'T just wear what everyone else has on. Go with what *you* like!
DO pay attention to the weather – floor-skimming jeans may be your style, but on a rainy day they will be soaked in seconds.
DON'T kill the impact of your outfit with too much jewellery.
DO avoid negative thoughts towards yourself and others.

BARGAIN HUNTER
If you want to ensure a totally unique, completely personalised image, turn your attention to markets, charity shops and car boot sales. You can pick up retro fashions that no one else will be wearing.

espina Pilavakis

Stacey Soloman

Project A

FASHION SECRET
Whether you're rocking the audience, strutting on stage or breaking hearts with a ballad, the little black dress is one fashion staple that will never fail.

COLOUR CLEVER
Make sure the colours you choose fit with your image and singing style. Every colour you wear sends a message. Natural colours such as brown and russet give an approachable, down-to-earth impression. Baby pink will make you appear feminine and delicate. Think about the message you want to send and the colours that suit you.

FASHION TIP
If you love animal-print fabric, remember that less is more! Accent your outfit with an animal-print scarf or killer heels. The all-over-body animal-print look is a no-no!

BREAK THE RULES
Remember that rules were made to be broken – and that includes everything you've just read here! If you have that mysterious X Factor, you just might be able to turn up to your audition wearing a bin bag and make it look fabulous. But it's a risk, and don't forget that in order to break the rules, you have to know what they are! So make sure you know your fashion basics, and then let your creativity take over . . . !

BLACK
Authority
Power
Stability
Strength
Intelligence

WHITE
Purity
Cleanliness
Safety
Creativity

SILVER
Star quality
Strength
Helpfulness
Dependability

RED
Energy
Life
Movement
Excitement

PINK
Love
Romance
Gentleness
Calmness

BLUE
Dependability
Wisdom
Loyalty
Calmness

GREEN
Growth
Nature
Luck
Generosity
Harmony
Energy

YELLOW
Laughter
Happiness
Optimism
Promise

ORANGE
Flamboyance
Fun
Happiness
Energy
Warmth
Ambition

PURPLE
Royalty
Wealth
Prosperity
Sophistication
Mystery
Wisdom

BROWN
Reliability
Stability
Friendship
Naturalness

Daniel Fox

Olly Murs

Lloyd Daniels

AUDITION TIP
Think about what you are going to say before and after your performance. The Judges want to know about your personality as well as your talent!

Vocals

You've got the look, you've got the outfit, but don't forget to ensure that you're pitch perfect on the day!

Ethan Boroain

Jamie Archer

De-Tour

"The standard is HIGHER!"
Louis

SINGING SECRET
Exercise your voice. That doesn't just mean that you should sing your audition song in the shower every day! There are voice-training exercises that create muscle movements that a song never can.

VOCAL DOS AND DON'TS

DO use your lips and teeth, and the tip of your tongue, to articulate your words as you sing.

DON'T strain your voice by singing too high or too low.

DO loosen your jaw before your performance. Stretch your face and jaw muscles. You will not sing at your best if your jaw is tense.

DON'T hold your breath while singing. The airflow created by your breathing creates and carries your vocal tone.

DO open your mouth wider to achieve a stronger vocal tone.

DON'T allow a negative attitude to let you down. When you sing, you wear your heart on your sleeve. If your attitude is nasty or negative, the audience simply won't warm to you.

DO learn to lift your diaphragm when you sing. A good vocal coach will help you, and you will find that your control improves incredibly.

DON'T sing if it hurts to swallow. Ignoring a sore throat is abusing your voice.

Olly Murs

Rachel Adedeji

Joseph McElderry

AUDITION TIP
Perform to the audience. This will allow the Judges to see your performance skills in front of a live crowd.

PREPARATION

• Learn from the best. Who's your vocal hero? Watch them in performance. What's their technique? Think about how they use their body, and how they present themselves on stage.

• Train in front of a mirror to spot the things you are doing wrong . . . and right!

• Play around with the size and shape of your mouth when you sing. You'll hear changes in the sound of your voice, and this will help you to find your own unique voice.

• Plan your performance to include high notes and low notes. It should have an introduction, a middle and a conclusion. Don't just sing as powerfully as you can from the start.

• Karaoke is a great way to practise your audition piece – as well as being a fantastic dress rehearsal for performing in front of a crowd of thousands!

Danyl Johnson

AT THE AUDITION

• Do drink room-temperature water as often as you can to keep hydrated.

• Just before your audition begins, visualise yourself hitting every note perfectly and sounding like a professional!

• Have the confidence to really *perform* your song. There should be a visible emotional connection with the song. The Judges will see the emotion on your face and in your body.

Nicole Lawrence

SINGING TIP
Feel the emotion. Singing is acting with music – if you don't feel the heart of the song, you won't convince the Judges that you really mean it. Get emotionally involved with the lyrics!

• Don't let the Judges see you sweat. If you sing with confidence, you may be able to get away with a few wobbles. If you stop singing the minute you make a mistake, you're sunk!

• Get the BIG notes right. The Judges will be waiting to see if you can hit the notes that everyone remembers, and you mustn't miss your chance! Don't focus on a single note – focus on the whole section. Changing the way you sing the notes leading up to the big one can make a huge difference.

Nicole Jackson

AUDITION TIP
Stand tall! Avoid slouching when you walk onstage.

Fact File

x

Name: **Alexandra Burke**
Home town: **London**
Mentor: **Cheryl**
Departure week:
Final – Winner

Xtra Access:
((SERIES 5))

 By series 5, *The X Factor* was hitting UK screens in spectacular style. Cheryl Cole joined the judging panel and injected extra glamour and energy into the show.

As well as the new addition to the judging panel, there was a brand-new presenter of *The Xtra Factor*. Bubbly Holly Willoughby joined the team and the crowds at the auditions were chanting her name as eagerly as they chanted the names of their favourite Judges!

Fact File

x

Name: **Eoghan Quigg**
Home town: **Dungiven**
Mentor: **Simon**
Departure week: **10**

Fact File
x

Name: **JLS**
Home town: **London, Peterborough**
Mentor: **Louis**
Departure week: **Final – Runner-up**

The X Factor was well known on a global level, and some huge international singers appeared on the live shows, including Mariah Carey, Beyoncé, Britney Spears and *The X Factor's* very own Leona Lewis!

Each star-studded live show attracted millions of viewers, and the voting lines were red-hot as people strived to keep their favourites in the competition. An extra innovation for this series was that acts in the bottom-two showdown sang a new song that they chose themselves, rather than ⌄

Fact File
x

Name: **Scott Bruton**
Home town: **Manchester**
Mentor: **Simon**
Departure week: **3**

Fact File
x

Name: **Ruth Lorenzo**
Home town: **Murcia, Spain**
Mentor: **Dannii**
Departure week: **8**

Fact File
✕

Name: **Austin Drage**
Home town: **Grays**
Mentor: **Simon**
Departure week: **4**

repeating the song they performed in the first part of the show.

The twelve finalists were a close-knit group. They even recorded a version of 'Hero' with proceeds going to the Help for Heroes charity. The single went straight to number one in the charts! ☺

Fact File
✕

Name: **Diana Vickers**
Home town: **Accrington**
Mentor: **Cheryl**
Departure week: **9**

Fact File
✕

Name: **Rachel Hylton**
Home town: **London**
Mentor: **Dannii**
Departure week: **7**

Fact File
✕

Name: **Laura White**
Home town: **Atherton**
Mentor: **Cheryl**
Departure week: **5**

Plus...
Girlband, Daniel Evans & Bad Lashes

THE X FACTOR

SERIES 5: 2008 WINNER

Alexandra BURKE

Alexandra Burke started singing when she was five, but until she auditioned for *The X Factor* she had had no vocal training and was working as a singer at weekends in clubs, dreaming of stardom.

She first auditioned for *The X Factor* in 2005, but didn't make it through to the live shows. However, she was determined to make her dreams come true, and in 2008 she decided that it was time to try again.

Audition

Alexandra was nineteen when she stood in front of the Judges for the second time. The memories of her previous disappointment haunted her, and made her very nervous. She could only hope that the Judges would see the changes she had gone through in the three years since her first audition.

Alexandra felt that she had learnt a lot and grown up as a person, but now she had to hope that the Judges would see that too. Conquering her nerves, Alexandra took a deep breath... and gave an amazing performance!

The live performances

Cheryl became Alexandra's mentor and chose to put her through to the live shows, where she staggered the Judges with her voice, her style and her choreography. Everyone agreed

"You are WORLD CLASS!"

Louis

WINNER
ALEXANDRA BURKE

that her first performance was tremendous. She went from strength to strength, and the audience loved her.

The pressure intensified as the weeks progressed and Alexandra met every challenge head-on. Her confidence grew and she began to shine like a true diva. It was clear that she had the elusive X Factor! ⤵

"A **FAULTLESS** performance!"
Dannii

Fact File

Name: **Alexandra Imelda Cecelia Ewan Burke**
Date of Birth: **25/08/1988**
Home Town: **London**
Singing Style: **R&B, Pop & Soul**

WINNER
ALEXANDRA BURKE

Week after week Alexandra delivered show-stopping numbers and had incredible experiences, including meeting and singing to her idol, Mariah Carey. Despite her continuing nerves and self-doubt, she was consistently tremendous, enthusiastic and good-natured. She won a deserved place in the final!

"**This girl is on FIRE!**"

Cheryl

*WINNING SONG LIST

1.	**I Wanna Dance With Somebody**
2.	**I'll Be There**
3.	**Candyman**
4.	**On The Radio**
5.	**Without You**
6.	**You Are So Beautiful**
7.	**Relight My Fire**
8.	**Toxic**
9.	**Listen**
10.	**Don't Stop the Music**
11.	**Unbreak My Heart**
12.	**Silent Night**

The Final

Under Cheryl's guidance, Alexandra stormed through to the final where she performed a fantastic duet with another of her idols, Beyoncé. The cheers of the crowd were deafening and Alexandra was overwhelmed as her hero praised her electrifying performance.

Alexandra was lost for words when she was declared the winner. Her career as a singing superstar had begun!

What Happened Next?

Alexandra has had a sensational year since being crowned *The X Factor* champion in 2008. Her first single, *Hallelujah*, became the Christmas number one and the fastest-selling single by a female artist in UK chart history. She has headlined the sell-out *X Factor Live Tour*, begun work on her debut album and recorded across the globe. Alexandra's future is glittering! ☺

"**I'm living MY dream!**"
Alexandra

Xtra Access: ((SERIES 4))

After the explosive success of the third series of *The X Factor*, everyone was wondering how series four could get any more exciting. The answer was simple – a huge shake-up of the format! A fourth Judge was added to the panel, the minimum age for applicants was lowered and the number of categories went from three to four. *The X Factor* hit the headlines before recording even began!

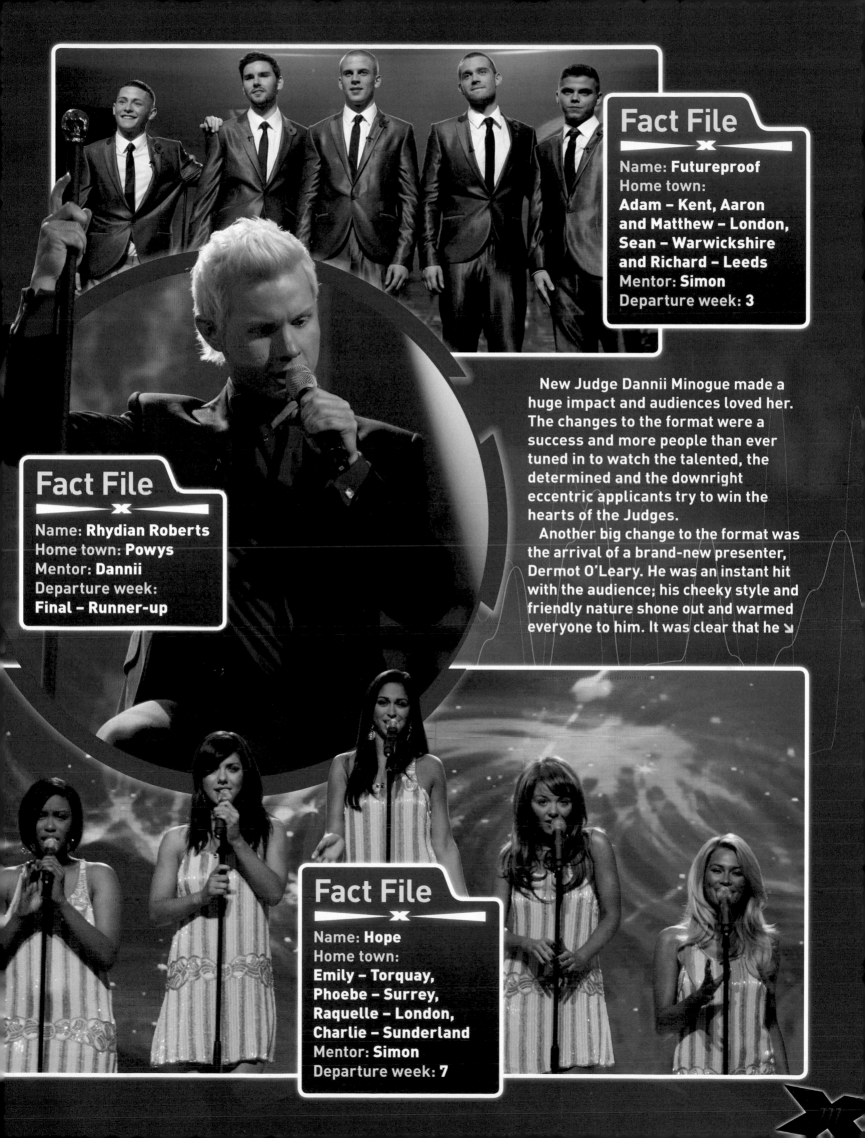

Fact File

x

Name: **Futureproof**
Home town:
**Adam – Kent, Aaron
and Matthew – London,
Sean – Warwickshire
and Richard – Leeds**
Mentor: **Simon**
Departure week: **3**

Fact File

x

Name: **Rhydian Roberts**
Home town: **Powys**
Mentor: **Dannii**
Departure week:
Final – Runner-up

New Judge Dannii Minogue made a
huge impact and audiences loved her.
The changes to the format were a
success and more people than ever
tuned in to watch the talented, the
determined and the downright
eccentric applicants try to win the
hearts of the Judges.

Another big change to the format was
the arrival of a brand-new presenter,
Dermot O'Leary. He was an instant hit
with the audience; his cheeky style and
friendly nature shone out and warmed
everyone to him. It was clear that he ➘

Fact File

x

Name: **Hope**
Home town:
**Emily – Torquay,
Phoebe – Surrey,
Raquelle – London,
Charlie – Sunderland**
Mentor: **Simon**
Departure week: **7**

Fact File
❌

Name: **Daniel DeBourg**
Home town: **Chelmsford**
Mentor: **Louis**
Departure week: **2**

Fact File
❌

Name: **Niki Evans**
Home town: **Polesworth**
Mentor: **Louis**
Departure week: **8**

empathised with the nervous people waiting to audition, and he was just as pleased as them when the auditions went well!

By the time of the Judges' Houses stage, the pressure was more intense than ever before. Each Judge was determined to win, brimming with confidence in the acts they had chosen. The live shows were about to start, and the contestants were preparing for the chance of a lifetime. It was shaping up to be a dramatic series! ○

Fact File
❌

Name:
Beverley Trotman
Home town: **Luton**
Mentor: **Louis**
Departure week: **6**

Fact File
❌

Name: **Alisha Bennett**
Home town: **London**
Mentor: **Sharon**
Departure week: **5**

Plus...
Kimberley Southwick

Leon JACKSON

Leon is an only child and was bought up by his mum in West Lothian. He has always loved contemporary jazz and singing, and in 2007 he got up the courage to audition for the *The X Factor*.

The journey of this shy young man from his nervous first audition to his resounding triumph in the final touched the hearts of everyone who watched him.

Audition

Leon's dream was to be as successful as his hero, Michael Bublé. But when he arrived alone for his audition, he was unconfident and uncertain of himself. His mouth was dry as he stood in front of the Judges.
He took a deep breath... and sang.

The Judges knew that he was scared, but they also knew that he had something special. Tears were in Leon's eyes as they voted him through to the next round!

Dannii became Leon's mentor, and put him through to the live shows.

The live performances

When the live shows began, Leon felt completely out of his depth. He had a disastrous first week because of his nerves, but as time went on he showed that he could do better . . . much better! The audience warmed to Leon's vulnerability, and the public vote carried him through.

"This means the WORLD to me."
- Leon

WINNER

LEON JACKSON

As his confidence grew, the showman within him began to perform. He got better and better, and halfway through the series his turning point was with the classic song 'You Don't Know Me'. For the first time, Leon really felt that he belonged onstage.↘

"Scotland should be PROUD of you!"
Louis

Fact File
×

Name: **Leon Jackson**
Date of Birth:
30/12/1988
Home Town:
West Lothian
Singing Style:
Adult Contemporary, Pop, Jazz

LEON JACKSON

By the time he reached the semi-final, Leon was really daring to believe in himself. With Dannii's guidance, he made it through to the final!

"It's been the most INCREDIBLE experience of my whole life."

Leon

The Final

In the final, Leon performed a duet with Kylie Minogue and sang like a true professional. His passion for music shone out in his final performances, and the audience cheered and applauded. Everyone was hoping that the shy Scottish boy would be able to make his dreams come true!

The audience at home voted in their millions, and against all the odds, Leon won the coveted recording contract with Simon Cowell's company Syco.

What Happened Next?

After winning *The X Factor*, Leon's life completely changed. He had the fastest-selling single of the year with his first release, 'When You Believe'. He headlined the massive *The X Factor* arena tour across the UK, and his first album was recorded with a variety of world-class producers. Best of all, he has performed at Wembley Arena with his idol Michael Bublé.

"Leon is a guy whose dream came TRUE."

Dannii

Xtra Access: ((SERIES 3))

The third series of *The X Factor* was the most dynamic yet. More people auditioned than ever before, and Simon Cowell was looking for a world-class act. After two series it was clear that *The X Factor* attracted some of the best talent the UK had to offer. The search was on for a star who could stand on the world stage.

Music truly does bring people together. *The X Factor* has created many lasting friendships. Groups have even been put together while people queued up for their audition!

Fact File

Name: Eton Road
Home town: Liverpool
Mentor: Louis
Departure week: 7

Only those who are going through the same experience can really understand how it feels to get through to the Bootcamp stage after their audition. Riding high on the crest of a wave, successful applicants burst out of the audition room bubbling with excitement . . . but there is a long road ahead of them.

To make it through the high-pressure environment of Bootcamp requires not only talent but also determination, dedication and strength of character. If someone can't cope with the criticism at this ⌐

Fact File

Name: Kerry McGregor
Home town:
West Lothian
Mentor: Sharon
Departure week: 3

Fact File

Name: Ray Quinn
Home town: Liverpool
Mentor: Simon
Departure week:
Final – Runner-up

Fact File
x

Name: **Ashley McKenzie**
Home town: **Croydon**
Mentor: **Simon**
Departure week: **4**

stage, how will they react in front of a live audience? Pulses raced and adrenaline pumped as the number of successful applicants dwindled. As Bootcamp drew to a close, a lucky few would spend one-to-one time with their mentors.

Fact File
x

Name: **Robert Allen**
Home town: **Essex**
Mentor: **Sharon**
Departure week: **6**

Fact File
x

Name: **Nikitta Angus**
Home town: **Glasgow**
Mentor: **Simon**
Departure week: **5**

Fact File
x

Name: **Ben Mills**
Home town: **Ashford**
Mentor: **Sharon**
Departure week: **9**

Plus...
4sure, The Unconventionals & Dionne Mitchell

Leona LEWIS

Leona Lewis grew up in London and always loved music. She trained at the Sylvia Young Theatre School and enjoyed writing her own songs.

Leona first trained in opera but went on to sing jazz and blues. Her idols were Whitney Houston, Mariah Carey and Eva Cassidy. Leona recorded two demo albums but neither were released, and she was starting to lose heart when her boyfriend persuaded her to enter *The X Factor*.

Audition

Leona was twenty-one when she auditioned for the Judges. She sang 'Somewhere Over the Rainbow', and the judges were hugely impressed. Simon and guest Judge Paula Abdul applauded! Everyone knew that

"Absolutely FANTASTIC!"

Simon

Leona's voice was something out of the ordinary. They all agreed to put her through to the next stage of the competition.

Leona sailed through Bootcamp and Simon Cowell became her mentor. After several tense days working with Simon and his team, she was chosen to take part in the live shows. She could hardly wait to get started!

The live performances

Leona's live performances on *The X Factor* were spectacular, and the whole of the UK was buzzing with her name. It seemed as if she could do no wrong!

Leona could hardly believe she was in the competition. Simon was supporting her all the way; he was certain that she could be one of the country's greatest solo artists. ↘

WINNER

LEONA LEWIS

"You've got a LOT of class, girl."
Louis

Fact File
— x —

Name: **Leona Louise Lewis**
Date of Birth: **03/04/1985**
Home Town: **London**
Singing Style: **Pop, R&B**

WINNER
LEONA LEWIS

> **"You've ALL made my dreams come true."**
> Leona

The Judges praised Leona's tremendous vocal range and encouraged her to have confidence and believe in herself. Her shyness overwhelmed her at first, but over the weeks she blossomed into an amazing all-round performer!

Leona's talent and determination carried her through to the semi-finals and won her a place in the final of *The X Factor* 2006.

*WINNING SONG LIST

1. I'll Be There
2. The First Cut is the Deepest
3. Summertime
4. Chiquitita
5. Sorry Seems to Be the Hardest Word
6. Bridge Over Troubled Water
7. Lady Marmalade
8. I Will Always Love You
9. Could It Be Magic
10. Without You
11. I Have Nothing
12. Over the Rainbow
13. A Million Love Songs
14. All By Myself

The Final

When Leona reached the final, her dream was within reach. One of the highlights of the show was her duet with Take That, who said that she was fifty times better than any other contestant on the show. The audience went wild!

Leona burst into tears when the results were announced, and Simon rushed on stage to congratulate her. She was the first-ever female winner of *The X Factor*!

What Happened Next?

Leona's first album, *Spirit*, was the fastest-selling debut album and the biggest seller of 2007 in the UK. She is a multi-platinum selling artist and three-time Grammy Award nominee.

Leona won 'Newcomer of the Year' at the 2007 Cosmopolitan Ultimate Woman of the Year Awards and was nominated for four BRIT Awards. She is living proof that *The X Factor* can change your life!

"Simply **SENSATIONAL!**"

Simon

Fact File

x

Name: **Journey South**
Home town:
Middlesborough
Mentor: **Simon**
Departure week: **10**

Xtra Access:
(((SERIES 2)))

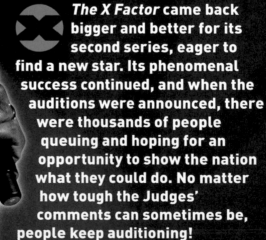

Fact File

x

Name: **Andy Abraham**
Home town: **London**
Mentor: **Sharon**
Departure week:
Final – Runner-up

The X Factor came back bigger and better for its second series, eager to find a new star. Its phenomenal success continued, and when the auditions were announced, there were thousands of people queuing and hoping for an opportunity to show the nation what they could do. No matter how tough the Judges' comments can sometimes be, people keep auditioning!

The show is the biggest television talent competition in Europe, and the chance to win a recording contract has brought people flooding into the open auditions. They wait in line for

Fact File

x

Name: **Shayne Ward**
Home town: **Manchester**
Mentor: **Louis**
Departure week:
Final – Winner

Fact File
×

Name:
The Conway Sisters
Home town: **Sligo**
Mentor: **Simon**
Departure week: **7**

Fact File
×

Name: **Chico Slimani**
Home town:
Oujda City, Morocco
Mentor: **Sharon**
Departure week: **8**

their shot at stardom, hoping that this will be their break.

Some stand quietly, heads down, hardly daring to dream. Groups huddle together, practising their harmonies. Others, surrounded by family and friends, are fizzing with excitement. Who will be the next winner of *The X Factor*?

Among these vast crowds are the faces that will become famous – thanks to the live shows and the huge popularity of *The X Factor*. Journalists will write about them. Fans will ⬐

Fact File
×

Name: **4Tune**
Home town:
Southampton
Mentor: **Simon**
Departure week: **2**

Fact File
✕

Name: **Chenai Zinyuku**
Home town: **Bradford**
Mentor: **Louis**
Departure week: **4**

Fact File
✕

Name: **Brenda Edwards**
Home town: **Luton**
Mentor: **Sharon**
Departure week: **9**

scream their names. Unknown faces will be catapulted into the world of celebrity!

It's not just in the UK that talented singers perform in their living rooms and dream of stardom! There are versions of *The X Factor* in many countries across the world. Of course, they don't all have the quick-fire remarks of Simon Cowell to add that extra spice to the proceedings! ☼

Fact File
✕

Name: **Maria Lawson**
Home town: **London**
Mentor: **Sharon**
Departure week: **5**

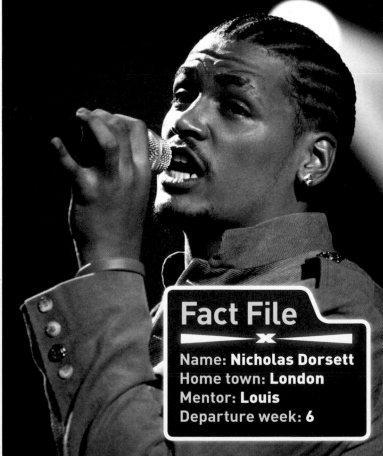

Fact File
✕

Name: **Nicholas Dorsett**
Home town: **London**
Mentor: **Louis**
Departure week: **6**

Plus...
Addictiv Ladies & Phillip Magee

THE X FACTOR

SERIES 2: 2005 WINNER

Shayne WARD

Shayne Ward grew up in Manchester and had always dreamed of building a career as a singer. Encouraged by his close-knit family, he made up his mind to seize the opportunity of a lifetime and audition for *The X Factor*.

Shayne won the hearts of the audience with his soulful voice. He was never in the bottom two throughout the whole competition! He went on to win *The X Factor* 2005.

Audition

Shayne auditioned for *The X Factor* in 2005 at the age of twenty. At the time he was working as a shop assistant, and he was very nervous because he knew that this was his big chance. However, he conquered his nerves and gave a great rendition of 'Sacrifice' by Elton John.

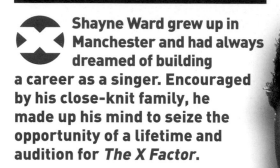

The Judges thought that Shayne looked sincere and confident – they were very impressed. They all agreed that he should go through to the next round.

"That was a FANTASTIC performance!"

Simon

The live performances

Shayne was hugely popular with the audience. His confidence and talent shone out on the live shows and everyone warmed to his friendly smile. Despite criticism from the other Judges regarding song choice, Shayne put his faith in Louis. Eventually he was the only act remaining in Louis's categories! ↘

WINNER

SHAYNE WARD

"I'm REALLY, REALLY proud to be working with you."

Louis

Fact File

Name: **Shayne Thomas Ward**
Date of Birth: **16/10/84**
Home Town: **Manchester**
Singing Style: **Pop, R&B, Pop, Ballad, Soul**

The pressure each week was intense. Shayne knew that he had to step out on the stage and fulfil his potential. With millions of people watching, that wasn't going to be easy! Through the live shows, his image and his voice developed, and it was clear that a star was emerging.

"I WANT to be in that final!"

Shayne

*WINNING SONG LIST

1. Right Here Waiting For you
2. If You're Not The One
3. Summer Of 69
4. You Make Me Feel Brand New
5. Cry Me A River
6. A Million Love Songs
7. I Believe In A Thing Called Love
8. Careless Whisper
9. Take Your Mama
10. If Tomorrow Never Comes
11. Unchained Melody
12. When A Child Is Born
13. Somewhere Over The Rainbow

"You DESERVE to win this competition."
Louis

The Final

Shayne reached the grand final, where he was competing with Journey South and Andy Abraham to be crowned as the winner.

After some incredible performances, the votes flooded in and Shayne won *The X Factor* 2005.

He could hardly believe that he had achieved his dream! Louis Walsh became his manager straight after the competition, and his career truly began.

What Happened Next?

Since his 2005 win, Ward has sold more than one million records, released an autobiography and performed a solo tour of the UK. His first single, *That's My Goal*, became the 2005 Christmas number one. Shayne is currently working on his third album. ☺

Fact File
x

Name: **Steve Brookstein**
Home town: **London**
Mentor: **Simon**
Departure week:
Final – Winner

Xtra Access:
((SERIES 1))

The first series of
The X Factor was
massively exciting. The
audience at home was introduced
to a new kind of music talent show,
and aspiring singers from all
walks of life were offered a chance
to make their dreams come true.
Crowds flocked to the auditions
and the atmosphere was electric.

Fact File
x

Name: **Verity Keays**
Home town: **Grimsby**
Mentor: **Simon**
Departure week: **2**

Fact File

Name: **G4**
Home town: **London**
Mentor: **Louis**
Departure week:
Final – Runner-up

Somewhere among the thousands of hopefuls was the future winner of *The X Factor*.

The concept was simple – would-be singing stars would perform in front of three Judges, and a lucky few would get the chance to perform on television. At the end of the journey, a wonderful prize awaited the winner – a recording contract and the chance to make a career out of their talent.

Many gifted singers turned up to the auditions . . . but there were plenty of people who the Judges had to turn down. Simon Cowell was already known for his sharp wit, and he didn't pull his ↘

Fact File

Name: **Voices With Soul**
Home town: **Luton**
Mentor: **Louis**
Departure week: **4**

Fact File

Name: **Rowetta Satchell**
Home town: **Manchester**
Mentor: **Simon**
Departure week: **6**

Fact File
x

Name: **2 To Go**
Home town: **Nottingham**
Mentor: **Louis**
Departure week: **3**

punches when it came to honest criticism! When the live shows started, audiences devotedly tuned in to hear the contestants sing . . . and to enjoy the battle of wits between the three Judges! *The X Factor* changed the face of Saturday night television and opened up a new world of opportunities for the singers.

Fact File
x

Name: **Roberta Howett**
Home town: **Dublin**
Mentor: **Sharon**
Departure week: **1**

Fact File
x

Name: **Cassie Compton**
Home town: **London**
Mentor: **Sharon**
Departure week: **5**

Fact File
x

Name: **Tabby Callaghan**
Home town: **Sligo**
Mentor: **Sharon**
Departure week: **7**

Steve BROOKSTEIN

Steve Brookstein was twenty when he discovered that his true love was singing, and decided to pursue a career in music. He threw all his energy into his dream, singing in bars and clubs, and working as a session singer. He had a number of disappointments with record labels, and it seemed as if his dream would never come true.

In 2004, Steve decided to audition for *The X Factor*. That decision would change his life forever.

Steve's Audition

Steve's first audition for *The X Factor* did not go well. He was finding it hard to believe in himself. He had been singing in pubs and clubs for over fifteen years, but it had always been his dream to make it to the top of the charts.

Steve sang well, but the Judges questioned his laidback attitude. At first they turned him down, but Simon Cowell asked him to come back the following day and sing again. This time, Steve sailed through to the next stage of the competition.

"It's been EMOTIONAL!"

Steve

The Live Performances

Steve could hardly believe that he had made it through to the live shows! With Simon as his mentor, he faced a battle to keep his position in the show each week and be in with a chance of winning *The X Factor*. ↘

"I am just so THRILLED for this guy."

Simon

Fact File

Name: Steven Desmond Brookstein
Date of Birth: 10/11/1968
Home Town: London
Singing Style: Jazz and Soul

WINNER

STEVE BROOKSTEIN

Steve's journey through the live shows wasn't easy. He faced criticism and even overcame laryngitis to perform on the very first show. By week two he was getting screams of appreciation from the audience, but not all the Judges were backing him.

Show-by-show, more contestants left but the audience had taken Steve to their hearts. He seized the opportunity to reach for the stars and made it all the way to the final!

"THE X FACTOR is getting me to where I want to be."

Steve

The Final

In the final, Steve found himself competing with G4, who were mentored by Louis. Steve sang his heart out and Simon was full of praise for him.

It all depended on the audience at home. Millions of people voted for Steve, and he won the coveted prize of a record contract!

What Happened Next?

Since winning *The X Factor* in 2004, Steve Brookstein has had a number-one hit, released two albums and performed to fans nationwide. After releasing an album through his Sony BMG recording contract, he went on to form his own record label. He is currently writing and recording new material.

"A FANTASTIC winner!"

Simon